CALIFORNIA'S
NUDE BEACHES

CALIFORNIA'S NUDE BEACHES

The Clothes-Free/Hassle-Free Guide

Third Edition

Listings & Photography
By Dave Patrick

Bold Type, Inc.
Berkeley, CA

California's Nude Beaches: The Clothes-Free/Hassle-Free Guide

Bold Type, Inc.
P.O. Box 1984
Berkeley, CA 94701

ISBN 0-9614880-2-6

First Edition: June 1985
Revised Edition: May 1988
Second Printing: September 1988
Third Edition: June 1991

10 9 8 7 6 5 4

Cover Photography: Dave Patrick
Cover Design: Mark Ziemann
Art Director: Mark Ziemann
Typesetting: Kay Nears and Boyd Hunter
Proofreaders: Uncle St. Nunzio and Carol Trasatto

Special thanks to Tim Baker, Jennifer Bickerstaff, Nancy Carta, Mary Deland, Miki Demarest, Tom McElheney, Colleen McEvoy, Donna Norris, Diana Purcey, Murray Spitzer, Kat Sunlove, Craig Trexler, Diane Valay and Layne Winklebleck.

This book is dedicated to my father,
Arthur C. Patrick (1923-1966)

CONTENTS

SKINNY-DIPPING SIDEBARS:

INTRODUCTION

H ave California's nude beaches, born during the taboo-shattering sixties, gone the way of love beads and bell-bottomed pants? Has the wave of censorship, which focused on the photographs of Robert Mapplethorpe and the music of 2 Live Crew in 1990, splashed on the shores of our free beaches? Now that Florida has banned the thong bathing suit, can a California cover-up be far behind? Hardly.

Although it's true that the circus atmosphere which drew crowds of 60,000 to Black's Beach in the mid-1970s is gone (down to about 10,000 on hot summer weekends), and even topless women are a rare sight at Venice Beach, formerly Los Angeles County's premier skinny-dipping locale (circa 1973–1974), the apparent disappearance of nude bathers is deceiving. In Southern California, many have become members at nude resorts, or spend their weekends at recently opened clothing-optional motels in Palm Springs.

Much to the delight of Northern California naturists, smaller nude beaches have popped up in rural Mendocino, Humboldt and Lake Counties. There's even a brand-new beach within the Santa Cruz city limits (Twenty-Two Twenty-Two), while the nude scene has re-emerged at San Francisco's Fort Funston and Monterey's Garrapata Beach. Why drive to a major beach when there's a nude swimming hole right in your own back-yard?

Attendance hasn't dropped everywhere. Many beaches are more popular than ever: Red Rock near Stinson Beach and Frankie & Dougie Beach on Lake Tahoe still attract capacity crowds. Get there early or you won't find a good spot!

If you counted every pocket beach and secret swimming hole between San Diego, Eureka and Lake Tahoe, you could come up with hundreds of bare-bottomed hideaways. However, for the purposes of this book, I chose to concentrate on the most popular beaches and commercial nude resorts, as well as a few personal favorites, bringing my total to 75.

In the "Recommended (In The Raw) Reading" section, I offer mini-reviews of a number of other publications which can help you find your special place in the sun. I've also divided the state into five sections: "Southern California," "Central Coast," "San Francisco Bay Area," "North Coast" and "Lake Tahoe Area," providing maps to help you plan long-distance skinny-dipping safaris.

NUDE BEACHES AND THE LAW

Although skinny-dipping has been tolerated along the coast for more than two decades, it's important to note that there are still laws against taking off your clothes in public, even in the wild, wild West.

In recent years, enforcement of anti-nudity laws has been minimal, but such unofficial approval may change at any time. Usually, getting caught with your pants down will only mean an order to cover up, along with a warning, but it could cost you a $500 fine and/or 30 days in jail. Citations resulting in $50 penalties are more common, but let the barer beware!

Fortunately, such problems are virtually non-existent north of Santa Barbara and outside the Russian River area, but it's important to keep a naked eye on local politics. For the legally timid, there are three privately operated, commercial nude beaches within a 90-minute drive of San Francisco: Red, White and Blue Beach; San Gregorio and Devil's Slide. I've also listed "Clothing-Optional Resorts and Naturist Clubs" where you're free to commune with nature, au naturel, on private property without problems from police.

If you're interested in changing the laws and creating more public areas for social nudity, you'll find plenty of similarly minded folks in "Naturist Community Resources."

GETTING NAKED FOR THE FIRST TIME

Unless you're already a veteran skinny-dipper, you may be surprised to know not everyone takes off their clothes at nude beaches. Many first-timers are understandably shy: Men sometimes worry they'll embarrass themselves with an erection, while women are often concerned with attracting gawkers or pesky Romeos. Female novices sometimes test the waters by going topless first. The truth of the matter is, the nude beach scene is sensual without being sexual and those worst fears are (almost) never realized.

More often than not, even modest newcomers peel off their clothes after an hour or so, but being nude isn't the only way to enjoy a great beach. "Clothing optional" means just that and you're under no obligation to bare all. However, you'll probably feel a little out of place surrounded by so many naked people. Wearing a swimsuit at a nude beach is like the Fourth of July without fireworks. It's simply not as much fun.

YOU CAN'T BE TOO OLD OR TOO FAT

Nudists come in all ages, sizes, shapes and income brackets. Social nudism is a family activity. There's no such thing as being too old or too fat to visit a nude beach. Nudity is a great equalizer, tearing down upper and lower class distinctions, which often act as barriers between people. No one jogs bare-assed wearing a Rolex watch!

Being a naturist means accepting one's body the way it is. For most people, it's reassuring to see that few have so-called "perfect bodies."

TANNING TIPS & OTHER BARE ESSENTIALS

Contrary to popular myth (and the current drought conditions), it does rain in California. Usually, winter is the wet season but fog along the coast during warm months can hide the sun for days and weeks at a time. More frequently, the classic summer weather pattern means fog hugging the shoreline until noon, burning off, and then returning at sunset. On some days, the fog never quite disappears, or only stays away for a few hours, so it's wise to carry a light jacket.

You can't do much about coastal fog, but you can usually find a place in the sun by going inland. Lupin Naturist Club in Los Gatos, for example, is oftentimes a sun-seeker's dream when nearby Santa Cruz beaches are cold and dreary. In Marin County, Hagmire Pond is a good choice when the fog continues to hang tough at Red Rock or Muir Beach.

Lake Tahoe on the California/Nevada border is almost a sure bet for hot days and clear blue skies from May to September. A 3½-hour drive from San Francisco, it's the perfect weekend getaway. For fogged-in Southland naturists, there's the Treehouse Fun Ranch, near San Bernardino, 90 miles east of Los Angeles.

Locating a sun-filled refuge doesn't have to be guesswork. At the end of most of my listings, I've included a phone number you can call for a weather-or-not report. It may also be some consolation to know that overcast skies are quite tolerable when temperatures are above 75 degrees.

Naturally, sunscreen is important to avoid a painful burn and possible skin cancer. If you're pale from spending the winter months indoors, experts advise building a tan gradually. Avoid the midday sun and limit your exposure to 30-minute doses until your skin darkens. Those with fairer complexions may have to be even more cautious. Building up a good base at a tanning salon before hitting the beach is another way to avoid the pink 'n' peeling look.

In addition to sunscreen and a blanket, there are a few other basic necessities. Since getting to many bare-bottomed beaches involves climbing down steep, slippery trails, suitable footwear is a must. Athletic shoes are fine, but leave your flip-flops by the pool. Protect your eyes with a pair of good sunglasses to block harmful UV rays, and wear a hat to keep your brow from overheating. Most nude beaches don't have food or refreshment concessions nearby, so bring a well-stocked cooler.

YOU OUGHT TO BE (NUDE) IN PICTURES!

One way to preserve your tan year round is to take a picture of it. Hopefully, the more than 80 photographs in this book will be a source of ideas and inspiration. The section "Naturist Photography in the Nineties: Loading Your Camera for Bare" focuses on giving you the technical know-how to make better fun-in-the-sun snapshots. Be sure to check out "Nude Beach Etiquette: Golden Rules To Follow While Getting a Golden Tan" to avoid a photo faux pas.

GOT ANY SUGGESTIONS?

Although every effort was made to insure the accuracy of information contained in this book, local politics and topography can change, especially during an election year or after heavy rains. If you feel this guidebook needs to be updated, contains errors, or that I've overlooked an incredible sunning spot, please let me know.

Dave Patrick
Bold Type, Inc.
P.O. Box 1984
Berkeley, CA 94701

SAN DIEGO COUNTY

1. BLACK'S BEACH – For more than two decades, Southern California naturists have enjoyed this modern-day Eden, the world's most famous public display of private parts. During the mid-1970s, as many as 60,000 nudists flocked to this then-legal clothes-free mecca on a single afternoon, easily outdrawing the area's top tourist attractions, the San Diego Zoo and Sea World. Although its "swimsuits-optional" status was revoked at the polls by a slim margin in 1977, the shoreline's skinny-dipping tradition lives on, with unofficial sanction.

Now, during hot summer days, you can expect to find Coney Island-type crowds numbering up to 20,000 stretched out in the sand. Activities include bodysurfing, body painting (a long-standing Black's Beach tradition), swimming, jogging, Frisbee, sand castle construction, and working on a tan. You should be warned, however, that state budget cuts have eliminated the lifeguards who were once responsible for more than 500 rescues each summer. The warm water is tempting and enjoyed by many, but it's also treacherous. So unless you're a strong swimmer, stay close

to shore.

In 1982, heavy winter rains destroyed the Broadway Trail, which leads down the 300-foot cliffs from the gliderport parking area to the beach. For a time, the path was blocked by a chain-link fence and "No Trespassing" signs, but the route has been repaired and, at this writing, is better than ever. Wooden steps and handrails have turned the formerly difficult climb into a much safer one.

The Goat Trail, just south of the gliderport, is the quickest way to the bottom — short of jumping, of course! It should be pointed out, however, that this rocky road has been labeled a "False Trail" by San Diego County officials and that climbers have slipped and fallen to their deaths. If you insist on taking your life into your hands, at least wear suitable footwear for the trek.

How To Get There: The La Jolla cliffs, which overlook the beach, are within walking distance of U.C. San Diego. From downtown San Diego, drive north on Interstate 5 (San Diego Freeway) and exit at La Jolla Village Drive. Go west about ½ mile to Torrey Pines Road. Make a right and look for the entrance to the Salk Institute on your left, just past the college. That's Torrey Pines Scenic Drive, which will

take you to the clifftop parking next to the gliderport. To find out if the fog's burnt off yet, dial (619) 729-8947.

2. TORREY PINES STATE BEACH – If you prefer a more peaceful expanse of sand than the volleyball and Frisbee-crazed area at Black's Beach, a short walk north along the shore will get you there. Since the beach from Black's extends for about a mile, you'll have plenty of choices for that perfect place in the sun. This area is quite popular with gay men, but women and couples are also part of the mix.

How To Get There: See previous listing for Black's Beach, but leave your car in the gliderport lot and hike ¼ mile north. Then take Indian Canyon Trail: It's not a tough climb, but there are no handrails or wooden steps.

3. SAN ONOFRE STATE BEACH – Baring your buns in the shadow of a nuclear power plant has definite symbolic overtones: humans in their natural state, contrasted by the eerie starkness of high technology. But one suspects nude beachers frolic here simply because this beautiful au naturel setting is close to home.

Unfortunately, it isn't always hassle-free. During the summer of 1981 and again in 1985, police made frequent

BLACK'S BEACH

Paint It Black's! Body painting, au naturel snapshots and parades for skinny-dippers' rights are just some of the activities at California's premier free beach, just north of San Diego.

City of San Diego
SWIMSUIT OPTIONAL
Area North of This Sign
MUNICIPAL CODE 56.53

sweeps, resulting in citations which cost "offenders" between $25-$50. Although it's unlikely such enforcement will
ever completely stop the nude wave, use this area with caution. Most of the time you can count on friendly lifeguards
to warn you when to cover up.

Don't let the binocular-toting Marines along the cliffs at
Camp Pendleton next door bother you. They're only keeping
an eye out for crafty peace activists who may try to infiltrate

Nuclear power plant north of San Onofre nude beach

the sector undercover in the nude.

On the plus side, the scenery is magnificent. The long,
sandy beach is ideal for beachcombing and quite popular
with local surfers. In spite of the rugged cliffs which tower
above the shoreline, access is easy, even if you're not a
great climber. Facilities include picnic areas with fire pits,
showers and restrooms. Day use fee, $6; campers, $14.

How To Get There: San Onofre State Beach is situated
south of San Clemente, west of Interstate 5 (San Diego Freeway). Take the Basilone Road exit, go past the San Onofre
Nuclear Generating Station and continue on to the state
park entrance. Travel south for another two miles and you'll
see "Beach Path #6," which leads to the bare-bottomed
sun site. For information on whale watching or a weather
report, call (714) 492-4872.

LOS ANGELES COUNTY

4. SMUGGLER'S COVE – "There just aren't any good nude beaches in the Los Angeles area anymore. If you take off your clothes, you'll either be harassed by a bunch of beer-drinking gawkers or you'll wind up in jail," claims a professional photographer from Beverly Hills. That's because he doesn't know about "Sacred Beach," as it's called by locals, which has been an undisturbed paradise since 1985.

Back in 1981, Rancho Palos Verdes officials began enforcing L.A. County's tough anti-nudity ordinance and they arrested dozens of die-hard sun-seekers in the process. Since this beach is one of the Golden State's most beautiful, it's fortunate that the purge didn't last long. The calm, shallow water is warm, a series of tide pools to the south are great for swimming and diving, and the 500 yards of sandy beach receive good protection from the wind.

How To Get There: This tucked-away Blue Lagoon is eight miles south of Redondo Beach, just off Palos Verdes Drive South, between Portuguese and Inspiration Points, one mile past Marineland. Since parking isn't permitted along the highway, you'll have to leave your car in the lot at Abalone Cove, which costs $4. Then it's a ½-mile hike along Palos Verdes Drive South, past the Wayfarer's Chapel, until you find a well-worn trail 50 feet beyond a sign with an arrow for Peppertree Drive. If you miss it and wind up at the Peppertree Drive bus stop, back up 100 yards. Curious about the water temperature? Try nearby Torrance County Beach, (213) 372-2166.

This photo, and opposite page, Smuggler's Cove

5. INSPIRATION POINT BEACH – At low tide, this location is an easy five-minute hike from the main beach at Smuggler's Cove. It is used almost exclusively by gay men (as many as 50 at a time), who spend much of their time exploring the rocky shoreline around the bend at Inspiration Point.

How To Get There: See previous listing for Smuggler's Cove, except look for the trail that veers off to the right, near the intersection of Palos Verdes Drive South and Peppertree Drive.

6. VENICE BEACH – For several years, from the late 1960s until 1974, this was the most popular skinny-dipping sanctuary in Los Angeles County. It was certainly one of the most outrageous anywhere until the sight of 10,000 bare bottoms proved too much for local authorities, who ordered heavy police patrols and hundreds of arrests.

Thanks to the 1984 Olympics, however, Venice emerged as a nude — or at least topfree — beach once again. How did it happen? Visiting European women, who take suntanning their breasts for granted at home, didn't think twice about doing the same thing when they visited sunny South-

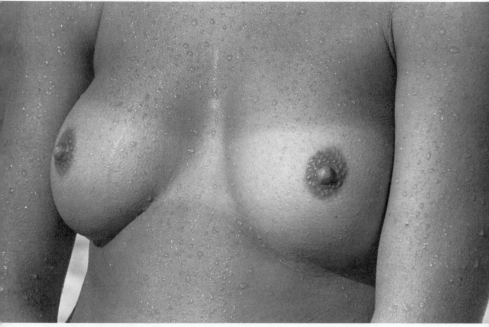

Ignoring L.A. laws at Venice Beach

ern California. Not wishing to provoke an international incident, law authorities simply ignored the fleshy exposure.

Since then, city and county ordinances have been used to drive away serious sun-worshippers (men have even been arrested for wearing T-bar bikini bottoms), but enforcement is erratic. Use at your own risk!

How To Get There: The community of Venice is located within the L.A. city limits, between Santa Monica and Marina del Rey. Turn off Highway 1 (Lincoln Boulevard) at Brooks Avenue, which ends at the ocean. Most of the nudity is sandwiched in the four-block area between Brooks and Westminster to the south. Forget about finding a free parking spot on neighboring streets. Pull into the most convenient lot and pay the piper, from $3–$8. To check on the weather, dial (213) 394-3266.

SANTA BARBARA COUNTY

7. RINCON BEACH – During most of the 1970s, Santa Barbara was the nude beach capital of the world. Blessed by warm weather and a thriving counterculture population of students and artists, the area boasted a dozen clothes-free/hassle-free locales. Unfortunately, utopia crumbled in 1978 when sheriff's deputies staged an all-out war on buff bathers, using both helicopters and horses to mount their

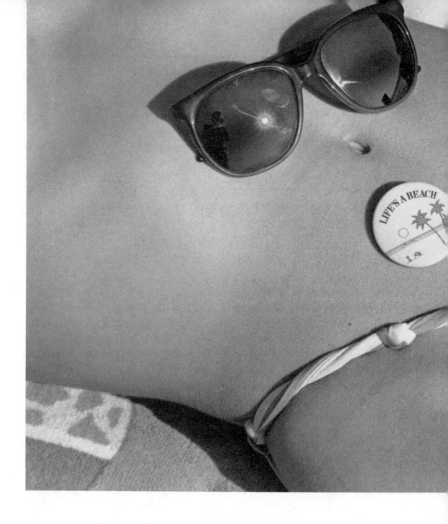

attack. Rincon Beach was one of their earliest targets, but
its never-say-swimsuit dream lingers on. The county park
consists of 2.75 acres, with parking and a picnic area, while
the actual beachfront extends for almost a mile. Thanks to
a new wooden stairway, the beach is even more accessible
and more popular than ever with both surfers and nudists.
Our only advice is to be cautious and do what the natives
do when it comes to taking off your clothes. If the sun is
shining and the heat is off, you should find plenty of well-
tanned tushes westward along the cement wall.

How To Get There: Rincon Beach is situated in Carpinteria, ten miles southeast of Santa Barbara. Take the Bates
Road exit off Highway 101 and follow your nose to the water.

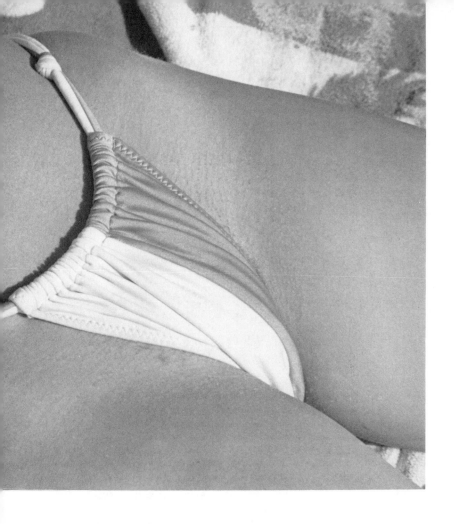

8. CARPINTERIA STATE BEACH – An emerging nude beach, this state park site has become increasingly popular in recent years, in spite of an anti-nudity ordinance passed by the city of Carpinteria in 1985. You *may* run into problems with the law at the east end of the beach, so we recommend staying on the west side of the large drainpipe you'll find there.

The *California Coastal Access Guide* calls it the "safest beach on the coast because of the shallow offshore shelf which prevents rip currents." Facilities at this 50-acre hot spot include lifeguards during summer months and a grassy picnic area, as well as tent, trailer and motor home campsites. Day use fees, $5; overnight camping, $14–$23.

How To Get There: Carpinteria State Beach is at the end of Palm Avenue in Carpinteria, not far off Highway 101. For a weather-or-not report, dial (805) 684-2811.

9. SUMMERLAND BEACH – Another long-time nudist nook, used as early as 1968, Summerland was raided frequently by police between 1975–1978. However, things have been pretty quiet ever since. Activities here include nude volleyball — just like in those nudist camp films from the

Summerland, looking south

early sixties — Frisbee, bodysurfing and pursuit of the perfect tan.

In addition to being easy to find, since it's just east of Lookout County Park, Summerland also offers an easy climb that won't take the wind out of your sun-seeking sails. Most of the nudity takes place a short walk southeast, past piles of steel-laced rocks placed there to prevent erosion of the house-covered cliffs. This area, near Loon Point, is popular with gay men. Before the age of AIDS, they had sex openly on the beach, but such blatant displays are no longer likely.

The clothing-optional sector extends for about a half mile, to Sand Point, so there's lots of leg room to jog along the shore. You may also have an opportunity to moon the Amtrack train as it passes on the tracks nearby.

How To Get There: Drive six miles east of Santa Barbara on Highway 101 and take the Summerland exit. Get on the frontage road, Wallace Avenue, and go ³⁄₁₀ of a mile past

Lookout Park to Finney Street, located just before the 101 south onramp. Turn right and you should find a place to park. For sun 'n' surf conditions, call Lookout County Park, (805) 969-1720.

10. MORE MESA – Easily the Santa Barbara area's favorite buns-in-the-sun site, More Mesa *has* had more than its share of police problems over the years. During the 1980s, however, authorities focused their attention on more serious "crimes." So, at least for the moment, More Mesa seems to have an unofficial OK.

MORE MESA BEACH

The More (Mesa), The Merrier: Splashing in the surf *sans* swimsuit, taking in the sun along with a good book and sand castle construction are all visible from the cliffs above Santa Barbara's More Mesa. But it's obviously more fun without binoculars.

In recent summers, attendance has dropped from 15,000 (circa 1977) to perhaps 1,000 during Labor Day weekend, but More Mesa still ranks as one of California's best nude beaches. Like Black's Beach to the south and Red Rock up north, a real community feeling survives at The Mesa. On a hot day, the beach almost takes on a carnival atmosphere, with jugglers, surfers, world-class Frisbee experts, musicians, dancers, joggers, horseback riders and volleyball champs. There's just about every kind of person you could imagine, except someone wearing a bathing suit. Be prepared for some walking and a steep climb; fortunately, there is a rustic wooden stairway.

Trail to More Mesa

How To Get There: More Mesa is located just north of Santa Barbara, between Goleta and Hope Ranch, three miles from Highway 101. Take the Turnpike Road exit south to Hollister Avenue. Go left on Hollister to Puente Drive and turn right. Continue on Puente until you reach Vieja Drive and turn right once again. Just past the junction of Puente and Vieja Drives is Mockingbird Lane, which ends in $^2/_{10}$ of a mile and connects with a dirt path that leads to the water, approximately ¾ mile away. Please note, however, that parking is prohibited along Mockingbird, and your car may be towed, so leave it on Vieja. For a fog check, there's nearby Arroyo Burro Beach County Park, (805) 687-3714.

11. GAVIOTA BEACH

11. GAVIOTA BEACH – You'll have plenty of room to beachcomb at this scenic locale, since the isolated coastline, dotted with spectacular cliffs and coves, extends for miles. Not to be confused with the beach at Gaviota State Park farther west, Gaviota Beach is a favorite getaway for naturists who prefer less-crowded surroundings. "Secret Spot," as it's also called, is on state property and never attracts more than a few dozen users because of limited parking along Highway 101. A faded, weather-beaten sign at the start of one trail leading to the water reads: "Clothing sufficient to conform to community standards to be worn at all times," so be sure to wear your birthday suit!

How To Get There: Gaviota Beach is situated 30 miles north of Santa Barbara, off Highway 101. Driving from S.B., make a U-turn at Vista Del Mar Road and go ⁶/₁₀ of a mile south. If you're coming from the north, go 1.2 miles past the Mariposa Reina exit. Look for the worn-in parking area on the right; another landmark is the SB-43 road marker, 50 yards or so before the lot. Cross the adjacent railroad

Gaviota Beach, north of Santa Barbara

tracks and follow the main trail, off to the right of several garbage cans and a screen-covered bulletin board encouraging litter-bugs to clean up their act. It's a short five-minute walk to the rock-lined shore. A number of other paths will also get you there, but you may learn the hard way why this beach is also called "Poison Ivy Point" (although "Poison Oak Point" would be more accurate).

SAN LUIS OBISPO COUNTY

12. AVILA BEACH/PIRATE'S COVE – Warm, shallow water that's great for swimming and snorkeling make this hideaway one of the most idyllic settings on the entire coast.

Pirate's Cove, as viewed from parking area

It's *so* perfect, in fact, that small boat owners anchor off-shore, swim in and wind up commuting to and from their boats on a daily basis, often for a week and longer.

The 100-foot cliffs overlooking the ½-mile-long beach do an excellent job of radiating the sun's heat, making it warm enough to visit, at times, even in December. During the summer, the population can swell to more than 1,000, with social activity centered on the informal volleyball games at the east end of the beach.

Incredible as it may sound, the police are actually friendly toward Avila Beach naturists, but keep a close eye on the voyeurs who peer over the cliffs (a.k.a. "Perverts' Point") at the south end. Members of the raincoat brigade, take notice! Pirate's Cove, by the way, is also known as Mallagh Landing.

How To Get There: Go south from San Luis Obispo on Highway 101 for six miles and take the Avila Road exit. Then head west on Avila Road for two miles until you see an uphill grade (Cave Landing Road) on the left marked "Not A Through Road — No Overnight Parking." Follow it and in $^6/_{10}$ of a mile you'll find a large, dirt parking area on the right, opposite the beach.

There are a number of crude steps cut into the soft clay paths that lead to the shore, but footwear suitable for climbing is still recommended. To find out if you should pack sunscreen, contact nearby Port San Luis, (805) 595-2381.

13. PFEIFFER BEACH – Even though you can create your own nude beach, river or mountainside at literally hundreds of isolated locations in Big Sur Country, Pfeiffer is the oldest and most frequently visited place to get down to bare-ass basics and work on a tan. As part of Los Padres National Forest, the beach is only open from 6 a.m. until sundown, but that should give you plenty of time to turn golden brown and enjoy the breathtaking surroundings. Of special note are the distinctive rock formations that dominate the horizon just offshore, which are accessible at low tide. Swimming, however, is not recommended due to the hazardous surf.

How To Get There: Finding this beach can be tricky. Drive south from Monterey for about 30 miles, then keep your eyes open for an unmarked dirt turnoff, just past the Pfeiffer Canyon Bridge on Highway 1. That's Sycamore Canyon Road, which also happens to be one mile south of Pfeiffer Big Sur State Park. Head west for two more winding miles and you'll reach the shore. Since the entire Big Sur area is known for its abruptly changing weather, a phone call could save you a fogged-in trip: (408) 383-5434.

14. ANDREW MOLERA STATE PARK – Much easier to locate than Pfeiffer, its country cousin, Molera State Park has 2,154 acres of splendid scenery, as well as camping for $5/night, although no showers are provided. The area is often too cold and windy for bare-bottomed use, but the rustic facilities *do* include firepits and toilets, which may be some consolation.

One major drawback is the lengthy hike (a good three miles or so) from the parking lot to the nude coves down south, which probably explains why this site draws only a handful of naturists.

How To Get There: The entrance to Andrew Molera is west of Highway 1, at the south end of Old Coast Road. Driving south from Monterey/Carmel, Andrew Molera is approximately seven miles past Bixby Creek Bridge and two miles north of Pfeiffer Big Sur State Park. For weather information, contact: (408) 667-2315.

15. GARRAPATA BEACH – Considered by many to be Monterey County's premier nude beach, Garrapata may eventually be destroyed by "improvements" such as restrooms and a parking lot now that it's owned by the California park system. Although years may pass before anything happens, a group known as "Friends of Garrapata" hope to stop the wheels of progress, or at least establish an area for clothing-optional use.

Why all the fuss over Garrapata? At low tide, the mile-long shore offers stretches of white sand, coves and caves, topped by breathtaking cliffs and mountains in the background. Certainly a beach worth fighting for!

For the latest information, or to find out how you can help save the beach, contact Friends of Garrapata, P.O. Box 1010, Pacific Grove, CA 93950.

How To Get There: Driving south on Highway 1 through Carmel, watch for the last traffic light in town at Rio Road (next to the Crossroads Shopping Center). Set your odometer and drive 9.6 miles where you'll see a worn-in parking area alongside the road. Signs warning "Surf Subject To Unexpected Life-Threatening Waves & Currents," "Climbing On Rock, Swimming & Wading Unsafe" and "No Lifeguard" are located near the main trail to the water, which is visible from the highway. Skinny-dippers prefer opposite ends of the beach, with clothed tourists populating the middle: South Garrapata is the most picturesque, while gay men usually head north.

16. ZMUDOWSKI BEACH STATE PARK – Vegetated dunes and a sandy beach make up this 177-acre naturist refuge. The path to the shoreline is steep, but an equestrian trail may make the trip easier for some. In addition to horseback riding, clamming and surfing are the most popular activities. Clothed users outnumber free beachers about 10:1 because of recent citations by park rangers, but its au naturel tradition refuses to die. Once known as "Hidden Beach," Zmudowski is now visible from neighboring homes and is patrolled by rangers who'll expect you to cover up. Use with caution.

How To Get There: From Highway 1 just north of Moss Landing, take Struve Road to Giberson Road, which dead ends at the state beach parking lot. Then walk north on the dirt access road that parallels the water. The safest place to be nude is in the dunes. Wondering about the fog? Dial (408) 688-3241.

SANTA CRUZ COUNTY

17. RIO DEL MAR/TRESTLE BEACH – Although nearby Manresa and Sunset State Beaches have all but disappeared as nude beaches because of development in the area, tiny Trestle Beach, just south of Rio Del Mar, has blossomed as an emerging clothing-optional zone. Don't expect big crowds, like those found at nearby Bonny Doon. In fact, you and one or two others may be the only ones nude among two dozen visitors.

How To Get There: South from Santa Cruz on Highway 1, take the Rio Del Mar exit. Driving toward the coast, follow Rio Del Mar Boulevard for a mile to Sumner Avenue and then turn left. Continue on Sumner, past Seascape Boulevard, until the road dead ends in about two miles. Leave your car a block from where the pavement stops. Hop over the train tracks and you'll see a wooden staircase, which leads to the beach. Your best bet for clothes-free, hassle-free sunbathing are the grass and dunes, 200 yards farther south.

18. SANTA CRUZ BEACH and BOARDWALK – In an effort to further equality of the sexes, a group of gutsy women, led by topfree activist Nikki Craft, took off their shirts in front of the Santa Cruz Police Station and demanded to be

arrested. They were not, and since that 1981 test of the law, women have had the option to go topless at the tourist town's biggest attraction. In spite of the potential for European-style sunbathing, bare breasts are as rare as parking spaces here, although both can be found on occasion.

How To Get There: Take the Ocean Street exit from Highway 17 and follow the signs to the Boardwalk/Municipal Wharf area.

19. TWENTY-TWO TWENTY-TWO BEACH – Although it doesn't offer much in the way of privacy, 2222 is conveniently located within the Santa Cruz city limits. Named after its proximity to a house at 2222 West Cliff Drive, nude bathers at this tiny pocket cove are visible to foot, bicycle and skateboard traffic on the sidewalk above the beach. Nevertheless, it attracts up to a dozen locals when the fog's burnt off.

Signs at the top warn "Cliffs are Dangerous . . . Remember! Hazardous And Changing Conditions May Exist. Be Cautious . . . Play Safe."

How To Get There: Take the scenic 2.5 mile route from Santa Cruz Boardwalk, past Lighthouse Point City Park, to 2222 West Cliff Drive. If you're driving south from San Francisco on Highway 1, go past the Santa Cruz city limits to Swift Street, then turn right and follow Swift to the coast. Turn right again and watch the street numbers. Should you

Twenty-two Twenty-two

wind up at the entrance to Natural Bridges State Beach, turn around and backtrack a few blocks.

20. FOUR MILE BEACH – If you'd like to try surfing in the buff without the warm, protective covering of a wet suit,

Surf's up at Four Mile Beach

there's no problem passing the undress code here. An extremely popular gathering place for Santa Cruz area surfers, Four Mile Beach is often littered with seaweed and surfboards. Now that it's part of Wilder Ranch Estates State Park, portable toilets have been added and the beach is cleaner than it once was, but park rangers began warning nude bathers to cover up in 1987. The threats, however, don't stop locals who have used this beach clothes-free since the 1960s.

How To Get There: Just look for the surfboard racks and VW vans four miles north of Santa Cruz on Highway 1. Leave your car in the unpaved turnoff area, cross the train tracks and follow the footpath to the beach. It's a pleasant ten-minute walk.

21. RED, WHITE and BLUE BEACH – With so many *free* nude beaches around Santa Cruz, it's hard to believe anyone would actually pay to enjoy the surroundings, but that's exactly what owner Ralph Edwards has been capitalizing on for more than 20 years. If you're a single adult, married or with your parents, he provides all the conveniences of a state park: picnic tables, fire pits, hot showers, a volleyball court and, of course, the option to run around in your birthday suit along 600 yards of coastline.

Cameras, guns, drugs and dogs are not permitted and walkie-talkie toting rangers keep the cliffs free of spectators. Admission to this artificial Shangri-La is $6 per single or

At right, the Red, White & Blue mailbox

couple for day use, or $8 (singles), $10 (couples) or $12 (families) for overnight camping privileges. If your idea of getting away from it all means playing strip poker while watching TV in a Winnebago, you'll love the place.

How To Get There: Red, White and Blue Beach is six miles north of Santa Cruz, west of Highway 1. Just look for the red, white and blue mailbox and follow Scaroni Road to the entrance gate. For additional details, give Ralph or his son Beaver a call at (408) 423-6332.

22. LAGUNA CREEK BEACH – Breezy, with little protection from the wind, the wide open spaces of Laguna Creek are nevertheless a strong attraction for the two dozen or so nudists who share this ½-mile-wide strip on hot summer days. The area is also a favorite hangout of fishermen and fully-clothed, beer-drinking voyeurs — but with so much

Laguna Creek

room it's not difficult finding privacy. Cliffs and micro-coves (barely large enough for a 6-footer to stretch out in) at the north end provide some relief from potential sandblasting.

How To Get There: Look for cars parked in the dirt lot on the east side of Highway 1, 6½ miles north of Santa Cruz. The main trail to the beach, which crosses the railroad tracks and goes through a metal gate, is opposite the north end of the parking area.

23. PANTHER BEACH – Incredible scenery provided by towering cliffs, striking rock formations and plenty of sand to stretch out on make this a *great* place to get your share of the rays. The environment is truly clothing-optional: some people wear clothes and others don't. Most visitors are young Santa Cruz-based hippies who also use the area for nighttime bonfires and sometimes set up camp.

At high tide, the most spectacular part of the beach — a good ¼ mile of coastline — is inaccessible, driving sun-seekers next to the northern cliffs. In spite of its beauty, Panther

Beach rarely draws more than 100 users, even when it's sizzling.

How To Get There: If you'd like to pay this quiet beach a visit, look for the cars parked alongside Highway 1, seven miles north of Santa Cruz. For a fog report, you might try Natural Bridges State Beach, (408) 423-4609.

24. BONNY DOON — Ask anyone around Santa Cruz to direct you to their favorite nude beach and chances are they'll send you to Bonny Doon, easily the most popular sunning spot in the area. Expect to join 200 others during the summer, with 90% topless or nude. What makes this site so attractive? Even on cool days, the horseshoe-shaped cliffs that overlook the beach offer protection from the wind

and double as a sun-reflector. Would you believe nude sun-bathing in February? It sometimes happens!

During the infamous October 17, 1989 earthquake — which destroyed much of downtown Santa Cruz — a man died here, buried under a cliff which collapsed, but Bonny Doon's strong community sense lives on. Although the sand is often littered with broken glass and other remains of late night parties, steps are being taken to correct the situation: The third annual Beach Clean-Up Day at Bonny Doon, sponsored by South Bay Naturists, was held September 22, 1990. For more information on how you can be part of the eco-action, write P.O. Box 23781, San Jose, CA 95153.

In recent years, social activity has revolved around the

Join the crowds at Bonny Doon

volleyball net where a friendly game always seems to be in progress. Nude jogging, Frisbee and frolicking in the surf are also frequent pastimes, although strong currents and hard-hitting waves make swimming a dangerous activity.

Some folks fear that Santa Cruz County supervisors may ban nude bathing on all but one of the currently free beaches in the area — Bonny Doon, Panther Beach, Scott Creek, Davenport Cove and Laguna Creek — but old habits are hard to break. It's my belief that law or no law, the clothing-optional tradition of Santa Cruz beaches, now more than 20 years old, will continue for a long, long time.

How To Get There: Bonny Doon is located at the junction of Bonny Doon Road and Highway 1, nine miles north of

Doon It Right: A contagious community spirit thrives at Bonny Doon, ten miles north of Santa Cruz, where nude volleyball, frisbee and jogging are popular ways to work on a tan. If your dog is well-behaved, Fido will be welcome and have plenty of canine company.

Davenport Cove

the Santa Cruz city limits. A parking area is provided on the west side of the road.

25. DAVENPORT COVE – Best known as a whale watching site, the tiny town of Davenport also offers clothing-optional recreation. Although it's not used as often as neighboring sites, there are usually a handful of free beachers at the smallish cove between Bonny Doon and the town of Davenport, where you'll find a walk-through cave and a spectacular rock formation just offshore.

How To Get There: Davenport Cove is just off Highway 1, ½ mile south of the town of Davenport. Driving from Santa Cruz, it's 9½ miles north of the city limits. Leave your car at the worn-in lot, go around a metal gate, cross the railroad tracks and a short, but steep, trail will lead to the sand.

26. SCOTT CREEK BEACH – A little known hideaway that's been attracting clothes-free visitors since the mid-1970s, this often-deserted locale is worth a visit. If you've been away from the sun all winter, you may want to make the change from pale-skinned to deliciously dark in relative privacy. You won't find many dogs, errant Frisbees or broken beer bottles here, but an offshore pipeline ruins the otherwise pleasant view.

At the north end of the beach, surfboarders and wind-surfers flock to take advantage of the waves created by a semi-submerged reef. In-the-buff beachcombers will love the rocky tidepools there, too, but nude bathers usually choose the southernmost section of this ½-mile-long beach.

How To Get There: Scott Creek Beach sits three miles north of Davenport off Highway 1.

SAN MATEO COUNTY

27. POMPONIO STATE BEACH – Although this beach has a long record of nude bathing on a small scale, its use increased dramatically in 1979 after being named as a possible "swimsuits optional" area by Russell Cahill, then California Department of Parks and Recreation Director. After his plan was nixed by Governor Jerry Brown, Cahill resigned, but in spirit, his move to legally free the beaches lives on.

During the mid-1980s, as many as 100 bare-ass bathers a day lined Pomponio's shore, but vandalism to parked cars along Highway 1 has trimmed attendance, mostly because police have blocked off the horseshoe-shaped parking area

Scott Creek Beach

just south of the state beach entrance.

In spite of difficult access and the problems I've just mentioned, Pomponio is a gorgeous, mile-and-a-half-long nude beach increasing in popularity once again.

How To Get There: Pomponio State Beach is near the intersection of Pomponio Creek and Highway 1, three miles north of Pescadero State Beach. You'll find buns-in-the-sun at the south end of the state property, an enjoyable 15-minute walk, but accessible only at low tide. A more reliable route involves leaving your car at the nearest pullover area and approaching the closed-off horseshoe-shaped parking area on foot. Then take the trail you'll find there. If you're worried about leaving the Mercedes unattended, spend $2 for parking in the state beach lot.

28. SAN GREGORIO – 1967, the year of San Francisco's "Summer of Love," was also the year this privately owned stretch of sand saw its debut as the first legit nude beach in California and the world. For more than two decades, San Gregorio's popularity has endured and it still draws 500 sun worshipers on a good day. Admission, which includes parking, is $2 per adult, but don't worry about the beach filling up; there's plenty of room for everyone.

In recent years, San Gregorio has been surrounded by controversy — and litigation — over public displays of sex. Defenders of the beach say the practice has stopped, but the driftwood structures which housed most of the objectionable activity are still being built. Once heavily populated by gay men, San Gregorio now has a mixed crowd, including families. Straights generally stay south, while the gays trek north. Pets are OK, but there are no restrooms or drinking water. Overnight camping, fires and cameras are not permitted.

Don't confuse this commercial venture with San Gregorio State Beach, one mile south, where you'll have to wear a swimsuit, although the borders between the two beaches have become somewhat blurred.

How To Get There: There are two access routes to the shore, each with a separate place to leave your car, but the southern entrance, a few hundred yards north of the junction of Highway 1 and Highway 84, offers the quickest and easiest path. The other entrance is two miles farther north; both are marked by red flags. You should also be aware that this site is often closed when it's cold or foggy, so a call to adjacent San Gregorio State Beach, (415) 726-6238, could save you a disappointing trip.

29. MONTARA STATE BEACH – Since horses are an occasional sight at this bare-bottomed beach, don't be surprised if you spot a modern-day Lady Godiva trotting by in style. Some regulars bring along portable protection from the wind, which can whip sand into your picnic lunch. Volleyball, jogging and Frisbee are the usual diversions. Although the coastline stretches for ½ mile, nudity is tolerated only at the north end of the beach, where voyeurs armed with everything from video cameras to binoculars perch along the cliffs.

How To Get There: Montara is off Highway 1, six miles south of Pacifica. Be careful where you park, however, since the CHP *does* issue tickets for vehicles left in the "No Parking" zone.

30. MIDDLE BEACH – For lack of a better name, we'll use the one the *San Francisco Bay Guardian* invented for its 1987 nude beach issue. If you don't mind a steep climb down some scary-looking cliffs, Middle Beach is a beautiful spot to tan your hide. It's also *free*, unlike Devil's Slide next door.

The coastal strip is bordered by towering bluffs that offer good protection from the wind, as well as privacy from other bathers. Unfortunately, this sweeping panorama of sand 'n'

surf also attracts more than its share of gawkers, probably because it's just a short walk from their cliff-hanging perches at Montara.

How To Get There: Middle Beach is simple to find. Just drive north ¼ mile from Montara State Beach. Early in the day, parking is available on the cliffs at both ends of the beach. Don't forget your mountain climbing boots!

31. DEVIL'S SLIDE/GRAY WHALE COVE – During the mid-1980s, winter storms threatened to wipe this historical au naturel setting right off the map, but both "Edun Cove" (Edun is nude spelled backwards) and Highway 1 have survived. Probably the most famous nude beach in Northern

The entrance to Gray Whale Cove

California, the clothing-optional legal battles ended here in 1970 when Jean Brunning went to court to establish her right to allow skinny-dipping on her own land.

In 1982, the area became state property, leased to operator Carl Ernst, who has made notable improvements by increasing the amount of paved parking and providing a Jeep, making the beach accessible to the handicapped. Included in the $5/person ticket price (children 16 and under admitted free with their parents) are portable toilets and hand-railed wooden steps down the 200-foot cliffs — a definite plus for klutzy climbers. Unlike most nude beaches, this one also has refreshments: a hot dog stand and soda machines. During recent summers, crowds have ranged from 200 to more than 1,000, depending upon the weather.

How To Get There: Driving south from San Francisco on Highway 1, you'll pass a weather-beaten World War II bunker overlooking the ocean about five miles south of Pacifica. On the opposite side of the road, ¼ mile farther south, is the asphalt parking entrance. If you don't want to take chances with the weather or road conditions, just call ahead: (415) 728-5336.

SAN FRANCISCO COUNTY

32. FORT FUNSTON – Just like rock 'n' roll, nude beaches in the Bay Area will never die! Although it's unclear why "Fort Fun" was ever abandoned, the jaybirds have returned to this naturist nook, popular during the seventies and early eighties. Unlike other nude beaches, it attracts most of its users on weekdays, when you'll find 20 or so bare bottoms scattered among the high dunes.

Swimming nude is not recommended on the shoreline below for two reasons: clothed families with children frequent the area and the water is rough.

How To Get There: Fort Funston is west of Lake Merced and Harding Park Municipal Golf Course south of the intersection of the Great Highway and Skyline Boulevard. WWII bunkers and tunnels abound in nude dunes, which stretch for a mile.

33. LAND'S END – San Francisco's first nude beach, born during the Sexual Freedom League days, was originally a gay beach that's gone more or less straight. The AIDS crisis ended the heavy cruising scene a few years back and now Land's End attracts sun-seekers of all sizes, ages and sexual persuasions. You may even see non-nude homeless people camped in the small cove at the north end of the beach.

In addition to a panoramic view of San Francisco Bay and the Golden Gate Bridge, you'll find large flat rocks to spread your blanket on if you get there early. Otherwise, it might be a good idea to bring along a foam pad to cover the rough terrain. Land's End can also be quite chilly, especially if the fog rolls in, so be sure to bring along a warm jacket, even in July.

How To Get There: Even if your budget doesn't include owning a car, that's no reason to deny yourself the luxury of an overall tan. You can visit Land's End by busing from downtown San Francisco (Muni #38 "Point Lobos") to the Ocean Beach/Cliff House area and walking north from Point Lobos Avenue on Merrie Way. When you run out of paved road, take your choice of several dirt paths down to the water — but watch out for patches of poison oak!

Should you decide to drive, Land's End lies north of Sutro Heights Park and west of Lincoln Park Golf Course, near the junction of Point Lobos Avenue and 48th Avenue. Parking is plentiful in the lot on Merrie Way. To make sure the sun is shining, dial the West Fort Miley Ranger Station: (415) 556-8371.

34. BAKER BEACH – Currently the most frequently visited skinny-dipper's haven in San Francisco, Baker Beach becomes a seamless quilt of bare bodies (as many as 500) on hot, holiday weekends. Naturally, being part of a sea of flesh has its own special charm — as long as you don't mind being a seaside sardine packed in coconut oil. If you're claustrophobic, one solution is to carry an oversized blanket!

Swimming in the cool, but calm, waters is a major activity. Unfortunately, there's no escape from the increasing number of gawkers in recent years. It's also often foggy and windswept.

San Francisco's Baker Beach

How To Get There: Baker Beach attracts bicyclists, who bring their all-terrain two-wheelers right down to the sand. From downtown San Francisco, take Geary Boulevard to 25th Avenue, then turn right onto Lincoln Boulevard. Baker Beach extends for more than a mile, just west of Lincoln. Parking is plentiful.

To find the nude part, walk north (toward the Golden Gate Bridge) from the main beach until you see someone without clothes. You may be able to park quite close by leaving your car in the northwest corner of the Presidio, near Highway 101 and the Golden Gate Bridge. For an update on the cloud cover, call (415) 936-1212.

35. GOLDEN GATE BRIDGE – There's just no stopping the nude wave, and "The City That Knows How" even has a free beach at the San Francisco foot of this famous bridge. Its location has no doubt sent more than one tourist scurrying for binoculars, but there's a better way: Join the birthday suit crowd yourself. Don't just dream about naked bodies, be one!

As you might imagine, the picture postcard look from this rocky vantage point is incredible. Because access is more difficult than at nearby Baker Beach, it's also uncrowded. If you're a good climber who enjoys semi-solitude when soaking up the sun, here's the place.

How To Get There: See previous listing for directions to Baker Beach. Then follow one of the steep trails west of Lincoln, down the cliffs from the Presidio, near Highway 101 and the Golden Gate Bridge. At low tide, you can walk north from the nude section of Baker Beach, but this route can be treacherous. Use either access with caution.

ALAMEDA COUNTY

36. TILDEN PARK – Although not an "official" site for nude recreation, one alternative to driving from the East Bay to Baker Beach, Devil's Slide or Red Rock is to simply find a secluded section in the wilds of Tilden and take off your clothes. When the coast is fogged in and thermometers in Berkeley are pushing 90 degrees, this idea can be especially appealing! It's a gorgeous setting with miles of rolling hills and greenery. Idyllic streams for skinny-dipping in the isolated wooded areas abound. In fact, several of the photographs in this book were shot at Tilden. Hikers often stumble across renegade sunbathers opposite the lifeguard/swimming/beach side of Lake Anza. Similar nude pioneering has been sighted at Oakland's Joaquin Miller Park.

How To Get There: All summer you can catch an AC Transit bus (#67) from downtown Berkeley to Tilden Park. If you'd rather drive, head up into the hills on Spruce Street. After crossing Grizzly Peak Boulevard, go east on Wildcat Canyon Road for about a mile. You'll find the well-marked Tilden Park entrance and a smaller road leading to Lake Anza on your left.

Nudes in Berkeley: Tilden Park

37. BLACK SAND/BONITA COVE – Off the beaten path in the Marin Headlands are two neighboring coves which offer striking scenery and an excellent place to commune with nature in the nude. Even on a hot day, the sites attract only a few dozen birthday suiters; on occasion, you may have an entire beach to yourself.

Black Sand, a.k.a. East Bonita, is the most popular beachhead. After reaching the parking area (see directions below), watch for a footpath that goes downhill to the left, near a Golden Gate National Recreation Area "No Fires" sign. Be sure to wear your walking shoes, since you'll have to make a 15-minute trek over terrain lined with poison oak to reach the shore.

From the same parking lot, the trail to adjacent Bonita Cove is downhill to the right. At low tide, the beaches are accessible to each other. However, keep in mind your return trip might be blocked by the incoming sea.

How To Get There: Visiting Black Sand/Bonita Cove involves a drive through Fort Cronkhite Military Reservation. Take the Alexander exit off Highway 101 north of the Golden Gate Bridge, then watch for the tunnel on your left leading to Gonzelman Road. Continue on Gonzelman, past McCullough. At the YMCA and lighthouse turnoff, go right. Soon you'll spot the Battery Alexander parking lot on the left. That's where to leave your car.

38. WEST BONITA/RODEO BEACH – Tagged in 1990 as the "Warmest Nude Beach" by the *San Francisco Bay Guardian*, this tiny cove disappears at high tide, but on windy days it's worth checking out.

However, there are a couple of drawbacks. In spite of a stairway, which takes you down most of the way to the shore, reaching West Bonita (a.k.a. Rodeo Beach) still involves a

East Bonita meets West Bonita in Marin County

dangerous climb. In addition, you should be aware that strong currents make swimming a sometimes risky proposition.

How To Get There: Same directions as Black Sand/ Bonita Cove, but take a right to Bunker Road off Conzelman Road. Past the Rodeo Lagoon you'll see a large parking area complete with a portable toilet, water and trash cans. A wide, dirt fire road will take you toward the ocean.

Muir Beach

39. MUIR BEACH – Erratic enforcement of Marin's anti-nudity laws has been a problem here in the past, but since 1985, County sheriffs have even stopped giving out *oral* warnings, making Muir at least a "semi-official" nude sanctuary.

"Little Beach," as some Marinites prefer to call it, is a quiet, relaxing place to enjoy the sun 'n' surf. But it can also be cold, foggy and windswept. The sun drops behind the surrounding cliffs relatively early in the afternoon, so be sure to get there before then if you're serious about leaving with your skin darker than when you arrived. And don't forget your jacket, even in July.

The nude part of Muir Beach is just beyond the rocks on the shoreline's northwest tip. The main section of the beach, however, is frequented by many picnicking families with young children and is *not* swimsuits optional.

How To Get There: To visit Muir Beach, just proceed north from San Francisco on Highway 101 to Highway 1 and watch for the signs. You can't miss it. If you're wondering about the fog, call (415) 868-1922.

40. STEEP RAVINE BEACH – You don't have to be a mountain goat, as its name might imply, to find your place in the sun at this incredibly beautiful stretch of shoreline. If you've ever enjoyed the fantasy of being stranded on a deserted island, you'll love the rocky, unspoiled view here. It's also an ideal setting for naturist photography if you or your model are the shy type, who don't want the attention of gawkers or other camera buffs. Used by only a handful of skinny-dippers and fishermen; even on a perfect day you may find yourself alone.

The descent is an easy walk down a mile-long dirt road, which offers gorgeous scenery along the way. The last

Steep Ravine Beach

hundred yards or so you can take your pick of several narrow foot paths to the water, but once again, keep an eye out for patches of poison oak, which often become overgrown. A favorite spot is the small beach to the south, which sits below a sheer cliff face.

How To Get There: To reach this sunbather's paradise, simply look for the "Steep Ravine Environmental Campground" sign on Highway 1, two miles south of Stinson Beach. You'll see plenty of "No Parking" signs on the ocean side of the road, but parking is available across the street.

To save your shoe leather and avoid the hike to the beach, rent one of the rustic cabins for $25/night or campsite $6/night (plus $3.95 processing fee for either), which also entitles you to the combination for the locked gate. Please note, however, that nudity is *not* permitted near the overnight accomodations. For reservations or more information, call (800) 444-7275.

A typical afternoon at Red Rock

41. RED ROCK BEACH – Marin's #1 site for nude recreation, Red Rock has a long skinny-dipping tradition that goes back more than 15 years. Like its name suggests, there isn't much sand on this smallish beach which is almost always crowded: You'll join as many as 250 fellow skinny-dippers on a hot summer day. Parking your car — or your blanket — can be a problem on a hot day. But, generally speaking, if you can do one, you can do the other.

Although the water never gets particularly warm, swimming and bodysurfing are quite popular. There's also plenty of other activity at Red Rock. Ultimate Frisbee champions, hacky sack enthusiasts, nude rock climbers, paddle ball players and laid back New Age nudists are all part of the scenery and were the inspiration for "Red Rock Review," a newsletter and video magazine published by Iris Bloom during 1985–1986.

In recent years, Red Rock's contagious community spirit

has been turned into community action, resulting in an improved trail to the beach with redwood steps and trimmed back poison oak. There's even a funky fresh-water shower and solar-powered "warming rock"! A great beach, with great people in a great natural setting.

How To Get There: Just leave your car with the others in the dirt parking area, ½ mile south of Stinson Beach and the intersection of Panoramic Highway and Highway 1. Then follow the winding path downhill to the water.

42. LITTLE STINSON BEACH – Sometimes confused with Stinson State Beach, where swimsuits are a must, LSB is a tiny strip between two coves north of densely populated Red Rock. Since it's tucked away and not well-known, Little Beach is a perfect romantic hideaway for couples. Large rocks, which make up most of the terrain, also offer privacy for self-conscious first-time nudists.

During the mid-1980s, sharks were frequently spotted feeding less than 200 yards offshore, but they no longer seem to pose any threat to swimmers.

How To Get There: Leave your car in the lot at Stinson State Beach, head for the shore and walk south. You can also simply walk north from Red Rock. For a weather-or-not report, contact the Stinson Beach Ranger Station: (415) 868-0942.

R E D   R O C K   B E A C H

Red Tails In The Sunset: Since the early 1970s, Red Rock Beach, north of San Francisco, has been Marin County's first choice for clothes-free recreation. Bare-bottomed rock climbing, paddleball, hacky sack and Ultimate Frisbee are a big part of most visitors' agendas.

43. BOLINAS BEACH – Since this spot is within walking distance of anywhere in Bolinas, it's quite popular with locals who slip away from their daily activities for an hour's worth of sun. Unfortunately, they like keeping a good thing to themselves.

Several years ago, the People's Republic of Bolinas went to extremes, forming a mounted posse to slap bare-ass intruders with a $50 fine and/or 30 days in jail. Nowadays, the sheriff's auxiliary is gone, but even during the week, when there's hardly anyone around, don't be surprised if you get nasty looks from residents who know you're not part of the local populace.

In spite of Bolinas' anti-tourist policies, the narrow sandy shoreline remains a favorite with many out-of-town sun worshipers, who ignore the stares and enjoy the beach anyway. The decaying remains of a wood and cement seawall provide comfortable niches for a lagoon-side naked lunch. Hit the beach before noon and you'll probably be able to violate some aging hippie's sacred meditation ground.

How To Get There: Drive north from Stinson Beach on Highway 1 for three miles. Just past the end of the Bolinas Lagoon, turn left and follow Olema Bolinas Road into town. You can leave your car on Ocean Parkway, which parallels Bolinas Bay.

44. RCA BEACH – Secluded and spectacular are two words used to describe this naturist nook, part of Point Reyes National Seashore. Although you'll have to be sure-footed to trek down the moderately steep cliffs surrounding this beach — as well as 10 minutes worth of trails through dense brush — its difficult access keeps the crowds away, making it quite attractive to many bathers. Like Limantour to the north, it's both isolated and undeveloped, but with the advantage of being closer to civilization.

How To Get There: RCA Beach sits four miles north of Bolinas, off Mesa Road. Watch for the worn parking area north of the RCA Transoceanic Relay Station and follow the half-mile-long cow pasture path to the water.

Sieroty Pond, in pre-drought days

45. HAGMIRE POND – Once upon a time, Sieroty Pond, just a few hundred yards north of where Marin County sunseekers now congregate at Hagmire, was Northern California's best old-fashioned swimming hole. Complete with rope swing and hundreds of regular users, it was the perfect place to float lazily in the sun when fog huddled along the Pacific coast beaches.

Unfortunately, 1983's heavy winter rains forced county engineers to pull the plug on this inland hot spot, which most folks simply called "The Pond." Rebuilding the dam officials destroyed is a low priority, so it's anybody's guess when "The Puddle" will return to normal levels.

In the meantime, many of its old friends have simply

moved to neighboring Hagmire Pond: nice to look at, but usually too polluted to swim in. There are also acres and acres of towering forestland that can provide privacy for discreet, hot, fun-in-the-sun lovemaking.

How To Get There: Go north on Highway 1 from Stinson Beach for about five miles until you pass Dogtown. A mile and a half outside the city limits you'll see cars parked on both sides of the road and a fence with a gate marked "Fire lane — keep clear." Hop out and follow the dirt path. If it's a hot day, you'll be able to see beachgoers from the highway.

46. SCULPTURED BEACH – Part of the Point Reyes National Seashore, this gorgeous, out-of-the-way location abounds with birds, seals and other wildlife. Naturists and naturalists seeking sun 'n' solitude love the rugged coastline which is dotted with gorgeous tidepools.

How To Get There: See directions for neighboring Limantour Beach and walk three miles south. If you prefer, hike in from the Point Reyes Ranger Station in Olema, a seven-mile trek.

47. BASS LAKE – California's drought conditions of late have turned "Bass" Lake, which has no bass, into an almost non-existent lake. However, it still attracts a small population of nude sunbathers, who apparently don't mind the three-and-a-half-mile hike over the often soggy Palomarin Trail.

How To Get There: Obtain a map from the ranger station in Olema, off Highway 1. Be sure to bring along your walking shoes.

The wide-open spaces at Limantour Beach

48. LIMANTOUR BEACH – If beachcombing in the buff is your idea of a pleasant way to spend an afternoon, then this is your kind of place. In addition to being one of the most panoramic stretches of unspoiled coastline in Northern California, the beach extends for some seven miles, making the area perfect to practice marathon running in the original Olympian style: *without* clothes.

At the west end of sand, two giant estuaries — Drake's Estero and Estero de Limantour — are teeming with undisturbed plant and animal life, since the locale is a protected preserve. Best of all, Limantour is part of Point Reyes National Seashore where nudity is tolerated unless it offends others. Complaints are rare, but when they happen, park rangers will help you find another spot.

How To Get There: Travel north from San Francisco on Highway 1 about 40 miles to Olema. Turn left on Bear Valley Road and continue for about two miles. Make another left at Limantour Road and follow it to the beach. Call Point Reyes Headquarters, (415) 663-1092, for information on current weather conditions.

SONOMA COUNTY

49. WOHLER BRIDGE/RUSSIAN RIVER – Between 1975 and 1978, this area became increasingly popular for clothes-free recreation. During its heyday, Wohler Bridge's ¼-mile-long beach attracted as many as 1,500 bare-bottomed enthusiasts. But the good times came to an end when one woman, a homeowner whose property overlooked the site, complained and brought fierce anti-nudity enforcement.

Because the police are no longer as diligent as they once were, Wohler is making a comeback as a nude beach but should be used with caution. A better way to enjoy this winding waterway is to rent a canoe from one of the nearby lodges and choose a more secluded place to strip down.

The fresh water can be invigorating on a hot day, but in some stretches the currents are strong. Unless you're an excellent swimmer, stay close to shore. Like most Russian River resorts, Wohler Bridge has a large gay population, but there are plenty of couples and children here, too.

How To Get There: Wohler Bridge is 90 minutes from San Francisco on Highway 101, north of Santa Rosa. Take the west River Road exit off Highway 101 and then Wohler Road north to the bridge. Leave your vehicle in the buck-a-car dirt lot and walk north past two large towers that sit in the water. The dare-to-be-bare bunch will be found a short walk up river.

50. CAMP MEEKER – A great inland location, free from crowds and coastal fog, Camp Meeker offers 50-foot-high waterfalls and two small pools to cool off in. Between tanning sessions you can also explore the surrounding greenery in-the-buff.

Don't expect more than a handful of other users, who may or may not be wearing swimsuits.

Wohler Bridge and the Russian River

How To Get There: Go north on the Bohemian Highway from the town of Occidental. After about a mile and a half you'll see a wooden "Camp Meeker" sign; continue north for another 1.8 miles and look for a yellow "Slippery When Wet Or Frosty" sign. Leave your car in the dirt pullout on the right side of the highway 50 yards farther up the road. A creekside path adjacent to the parking area will take you to the falls — a pleasant five-minute walk.

MENDOCINO COUNTY

51. GUALALA RIVER – Often cool and windswept, or shrouded by fog, this easily accessible site still attracts two dozen regulars when its wide, sandy beach is warm. Be aware, however, that the climate here is quite changeable: It may be perfect one hour and horrible the next.

How To Get There: Gualala River nude beach is located

Unspoiled & uncrowded: Lilies Beach

just across the Mendocino County line and the Gualala River Bridge, a mile south of the town of Gualala. You can drive to the mouth of the river via rugged dirt access roads on the west side of Highway 1.

52. LILIES BEACH – You'd expect all those back-to-nature hippies, crafts fair artisans and marijuana farmers who live in Mendocino County to have a favorite place to kick back in the sun, and this is it. Lilies Beach is part of Mendocino Woodlands, tucked away in a remote bend of the Big River.

Although it's all but deserted at other times of the year, during the summer months dozens of sun-seekers flood this hidden refuge for clothes-free fun. The setting is absolutely gorgeous: Most of the river is shallow and slow-moving, making it safe enough for young kids to play in, but there are also deeper pockets perfect for adults to swim and soak in. Not surprisingly, the crowd here is about half families.

How To Get There: Not as difficult as it sounds. As you approach the town of Mendocino (about 3½ hours north of San Francisco) on Highway 1, turn right on Little Jake Road and drive 4.2 miles east past a marker which reads "Mendocino Woodlands." A few hundred yards later, just before a "Weight Limit 9 Tons" sign, turn right on an un-

marked road, which is paved for a short distance and then turns into a dusty, winding dirt road. Continue for 2.4 miles until the road forks and then turn right. You'll see other cars parked under trees. The main beach is a 10-minute hike along a sometimes waterlogged, sometimes-driveable trail which parallels the stream and dead ends at a metal gate. Just before you reach the gate, look left between the trees for one of the most serene nude swimming holes you'll ever find.

53. BIG RIVER BENDS – Farther down the river from Lilies Beach is a series of sandbars and tiny beaches that are well worth exploring in the nude. Slip on a pair of old tennis shoes or flip-flops (to protect your feet from the rocky bottom) and follow the winding waterway until you see a site that suits you.

Don't expect much company once you're more than 100 yards from the main beach at Lilies, but if it's peaceful, natural beauty you crave, the Big River has it all.

How To Get There: Same as Lilies Beach (see previous listing), then simply follow your nose for nudes downstream.

HUMBOLDT COUNTY

54. GARBERVILLE NUDE BEACH/EEL RIVER – Not exactly a major tourist attraction, but this site is used by locals looking for a refreshing dip in the buff. Even when the mercury soars over 100 degrees, the water remains cold and draws only a dozen or so buff bathers.

How To Get There: From San Francisco, drive north on Highway 101 to Garberville. Take the first Garberville exit and then turn left when you see a "To San Francisco" sign at the first major traffic crossroads. Rather than returning to the freeway, go straight. After you start going downhill, watch for the first paved road, then turn right. Leave your car with the others, next to a pile of rocks.

55. BAKER'S BEACH – California's north coast is a place of almost magical beauty and this free beach on private land has become Sun King in the Eureka area. A popular beach for families and couples, Baker's (named after the owners) generally attracts about two dozen users to its smallish shoreline, which teems with animal and plant life. The climb down the cliffs is steep, but hardly treacherous. Come prepared with a good pair of climbing shoes.

How To Get There: Go north from Arcata on Highway 101 for 12 miles. Take the Westhaven exit to Scenic Drive, north. After a short distance you'll see a funky metal "Private Property" sign on the right and cars parked on both sides of Scenic Drive. During our last visit, we found a thoughtfully posted cardboard sign from the Bakers welcoming all.

College Cove offers an easy trail with wooden steps (above) and a gorgeous rocky shoreline

56. COLLEGE COVE – A really spectacular section of Trinidad State Beach, complete with a lush trail and wide, wooden steps for easy access. The ¼-mile-long strip of sand is even lovelier than nearby Baker's Beach, with large rock formations, towering foliage and crashing waves all adding to the view. Unfortunately, anti-nudity enforcement in recent years has cut attendance dramatically, now limited to a handful of bare devils during the week and never more than 50 on weekends. Still, for many die-hard naturists, it's worth the risk.

How To Get There: About 25 miles north of Eureka, take the Trinidad exit off Highway 101. When you see the sign for Trinidad State Beach from Stagecoach Road, go right. In about ¾ of a mile you'll see a dirt parking area and a sign for College Cove. The beach is about ten minutes away on foot.

57. WILLOW CREEK BEACH/DANGER POINT – Also known as "The Elbow," this beautiful bare-bottomed beach on the Trinity River doubles as a favorite fishing hole for many. Deep, fast-moving water makes it risky for swimming, but the area is often warmed by wind-breaking cliffs surrounding the tiny beachhead.

How To Get There: Go north from Eureka on Highway 101 and pick up Highway 299, two miles past Arcata. Drive east through the towns of Willow Creek and Salyer. About 2.5 miles east of Salyer, just past a rest area, you should see a funky dirt road marked "Dead End Road 6N51" on the left. Drive in about ³/₁₀ of a mile and park.

LAKE COUNTY

58. NEW LONG VALLEY – Next time you're in the vicinity of Clear Lake, here's a spot you might want to check out. The beach extends for more than half a mile, so explore both up and downstream for the best place to spread your blanket.

How To Get There: From the town of Clear Lake, drive north on Highway 53 to Highway 20, then turn right toward the Highway 5 town of Williams. Look for bare buns a stone's throw east of New Long Valley Road (Lake County mile marker 39.94) off Highway 20.

59. CACHE CREEK – An emerging site for clothing-optional use, Cache Creek attracts families with and without swimsuits. On a hot day, you'll find perhaps a dozen dozin' in the buff.

How To Get There: The beach is located beneath the Cache Creek Bridge (at Lake County mile marker 37.07) on Highway 20, seven miles east of the intersection of Highways 20 and 53.

CALIFORNIA/ NEVADA BORDER

60. LAKE TAHOE – It doesn't take too much imagination to figure out the unlimited possibilities for nude recreation in this gorgeous resort area. All you've got to do is walk around the lake, pick out a nice spot and drop your drawers! The surrounding wilderness offers hundreds of great hide-aways as well: You can bake your bones next to giant water-falls, tiny streams, or on the side of any mountain. Depend-ing upon the altitude, you may even have the opportunity to work on that perfect overall tan next to a hefty snowbank. Cross-country skiing in the buff, anyone?

Just be sure your bare bod doesn't offend anyone and bring along some sort of sunscreen. Those nice, hot rocks may be great for sunning, but in Tahoe's thin mountain air it's easy to get too much of a good thing.

How To Get There: Take Highway 50 from Sacramento until you reach the lake. Then just head into the wilds.

Lake Tahoe

Rock out at Frankie & Dougie Beach, Lake Tahoe

61. FRANKIE & DOUGIE BEACH – Even though the boulder which immortalized their love is gone, the nude beach named after the graffiti-covered landmark lives on. In recent years, Frankie & Dougie Beach has become the buff bathing site most preferred by locals and tourists in-the-know, who enjoy Lake Tahoe's crystal clear waters and outrageous natural surroundings.

You won't find much sand at this strikingly beautiful cove, but there are plenty of large rocks — some might be considered mini-islands — big enough for a blanket or two. Get here early and you may even find one with the right angle to the sun.

Precious spots in the sand at Frankie & Dougie

South of the often crowded main beach, stretching back ¼ mile or so, are a number of rocky perches for sunbathers seeking more privacy.

How To Get There: Go north from Tahoe's gambling mecca on Highway 50 to Highway 28, which winds northwest back to the lake. Five miles past the junction of Highways 50 and 28, leave your car (there should be a few others) and tighten the laces on your hiking boots.

Just off the lake side of the highway is a north-south fire road perpendicular to several rustic routes downhill to the beach. No matter which you choose, you won't get lost. Simply follow your nose to the water, a 15-minute trek.

NUDE BEACH ETIQUETTE: GOLDEN RULES TO FOLLOW WHILE GETTING A GOLDEN TAN!

The *New American Heritage Dictionary* defines etiquette as: "The body of prescribed social usages. Any special code of behavior or courtesy." Proper etiquette at a nude beach is not much different from good manners for other social situations. Once you give it a little thought, manners for socializing in the buff are just a matter of common sense.

GAWKERS, GO HOME!

Although it's impolite to stare at others, gawking at nude beaches is doubly frowned upon — especially when it's done with binoculars. Why create hostility and be the target of wicked glares, insults or perhaps a well-aimed stone? Rather than isolating yourself on an overhanging cliff or behind a distant sand dune, get in on the fun firsthand. You'll feel much more comfortable and may even make a few new friends in the process.

MAKING NUDE FRIENDS

There are plenty of opportunities for meeting people at a nude beach. Social activities, such as playing frisbee or volleyball, jogging, swimming and bodysurfing in the buff are sure-fire ways to have fun and make new friends. Pick-up artists be warned: The nude beach scene is more like a family picnic than a singles bar. Just because someone enjoys being naked at the beach doesn't mean they're looking for romance. Single men should go easy when approaching women who are alone — they'll let you know if they're interested.

SUN, SAND, SURF & SEX

Although an idyllic beach setting can be quite romantic, sexual encounters in public are considered uncouth by naturists. Putting suntan lotion on a friend's back, giving a nonsexual massage or hugging, all fall within the realm of acceptable behavior. However, prolonged kissing or erotic fondling do not. These activities are especially offensive in the presence of children. Even on an isolated section of the beach, someone may be inadvertently offended. Don't encourage voyeurs — save your bedroom activities for the bedroom.

Complaints about public sex have created problems at Pirate's Cove, Summerland Beach and San Gregorio. Let's not give the clothing-obsessed prudes an excuse to ban clothes-free beaches.

93

NAKED LUNCHES & LITTERING

Everyone loves a picnic and, as long as you keep the sand out of your sandwiches, you won't find a better locale than a nude beach. Just remember to leave nothing behind but your footprints. Let me go one better and suggest that you bring along a garbage bag and pick up a few stray cans, bottles or some trash on your way out. It's also a good idea not to use glass containers at all, since they may break and cut some unsuspecting person's bare feet. Don't let unsightly litter ruin the view.

CAMERA COURTESY

There's no law against using your camera at a nude beach on public property; nevertheless, it's still a controversial subject. Few will object to friends taking clothes-free snapshots of each other, but the sight of your camera may send some self-appointed censor into a rage. One way to avoid such confrontations is to shoot at isolated parts of the beach where no one is in the background.

Candid camera fans, take note: Using a long telephoto lens to sneak pictures is morally, if not legally, an invasion of privacy. Common courtesy dictates if you want to make photographs of someone, ask first. At Black's Beach, those with painted bodies rarely object when they're approached politely.

Permission isn't necessary, however, if you're making a scenic shot of the beach and want a few unrecognizable nude bodies in the background. At commercial skinny-dipping sites, cameras are usually forbidden, but some nudist camps — such as the Treehouse Fun Ranch — have special photo days.

DOG DO'S AND DON'TS!

W.C. Fields once joked that "Anyone who hates dogs and children can't be all bad," but both have their place at nude beaches. Although some state and city beaches prohibit dogs, they're quite common at most other locales. However, if you can't control your pet, please leave the pooch at home. Personally, I find nothing more annoying than a bounding pup running across my blanket, kicking sand in all the wrong places, or having a stranger's dog sticking its nose in my lunch. Owners should bring along a pooper-scooper or otherwise be prepared to clean up after their dogs.

PLAY BY THE RULES

At most nude beaches throughout California, there are few posted regulations other than parking signs and warnings for dangerous cliffs. Don't create problems by camping overnight where it's not permitted or getting yourself stranded on a false trail to the shore. Help protect and restore the local ecology by obeying restrictions on environmentally sensitive locales.

TOO LOUD CREW

One of the worst ways to destroy the peace and tranquility of a relaxing afternoon at the beach is to force others to be the captive audience of a loud portable radio. What's even worse is several, all tuned to different stations. Not everyone has the same musical tastes, so be considerate and use a Walkman-type stereo with headphones instead. If you're with a group of people and insist upon playing music loud enough for others to hear, go to a part of the beach where your party won't disturb others.

SOME FINAL THOUGHTS

In conclusion, let me point out that nude beach etiquette is just an extension of the Golden Rule: "Do unto others as you would have them do unto you." It goes without saying, for example, that you shouldn't play frisbee or throw a football where a bad toss could hit someone on the sidelines. If you accidentally kick sand on someone or crash into them while body surfing, apologize. In the event that the person on the blanket next to you would rather nap than chat, be gracious and leave them alone. Respect others and enjoy!

Loading Your Camera For Bare: Naturist Photography In The '90s!

Y ou don't have to spend a fortune to put together a memorable snapshot collection documenting your good times in the sun. Although excellent nude beach photography can be done with almost any camera, in recent years a veritable arsenal of weather-resistant, submersible and underwater models have appeared on the market. List prices range from $13.95 to over $800. Many are waterproofed versions of basic auto-everything models, but there are also sophisticated models for serious diving and professional use.

"Splashproof" cameras such as Eastman Kodak's Explorer, Olympus' Infinity II or Infinity Twin (with built-in 35mm and 70mm lenses), Keystone's Le Clic Tuff 35, Chinon's Splash AF and its cheaper cousin, the Splash GX, are designed to be used where they're likely to get a little wet, but not thoroughly drowned. These point 'n' shoot marvels are perfect for shots along the shore — and could probably take a wave or two — but don't push your luck!

For those who want to slip in a little deeper, without digging deep into their wallets, Kodak's Weekend 35 is irresistible. It retails for less than $15, including a preloaded 24-exposure roll of Kodacolor Gold 400 film! For developing, the entire package goes to the lab. If the idea of using a "disposable" camera goes against your ecological sensibilities, consider the wastefulness of trashing your trusty SLR by exposing it to an errant dose of sand and saltwater. Kodak has also demonstrated Earth Day concerns by instituting a program for recycling the cameras so they can be enjoyed guilt free. The fixed-focus, nothing-to-adjust camera is submersible to eight feet, making it ideal for snorkeling at the surface or taking underwater shots in your backyard pool. How good are the pictures? Assuming you want snapshot-sized prints and the lab does its job, they're just fine.

Minolta's Weathermatic 35 (with dual 35mm and 50mm lenses), Nikon's Action Touch, Fuji's HD-W, Canon's Aqua Snappy and Kalimar's AW-10 (110 format) are relatively inexpensive ($49.95 to $322) picture-taking machines with built-in flashes that can take a dunking and keep on clicking.

Nikon also makes the Nikonos V, the top-of-the-line tool for serious divers. It's built like a tank (good for depths up to 160

feet), has optional frame finders, interchangeable lenses (15mm to 80mm) and sophisticated TTL flash. The cost: a sizable $807.50, but it's available for considerably less at discount camera stores. A less pricey competitor, Sea & Sea's Motormarine 35, is depth-rated to 150 feet and features auto-exposure, auto-advance and rewind, a built-in flash and close-up mode. However, interchangeable lenses are not available.

I used an earlier model Nikonos (the IV-A, with 35mm f/2.5 normal lens) and a Nikon Action-Touch for some of the pictures in this book. Although many nude beach buffs are repelled by the sight of fancy cameras, these seaworthy companions attract a lot of favorable attention, especially when I go swimming with them. In fact, because of their novelty, I've talked many curious people into letting me snap their pictures. I imagine the same thing would happen with any splash-proof/water-proof camera.

If you don't want to buy a second camera for the beach, Sima makes a cheap (less than $20), waterproof vinyl pouch that will accommodate compact point 'n' shoot 35s. Ewa-Marine offers better coverage: Their soft housings, including an optical port for the lens, are designed to fit most cameras, including SLRs. Prices range from $49.95 to $159.

In a pinch, a plastic sandwich bag taped around your camera is better protection than nothing. Just be sure to screw on a skylight filter and leave a hole for the lens and viewfinder. At the opposite end of the spectrum, professional skin divers sometimes purchase rigid plastic housings, which control camera functions with external dials and switches. However, they cost as much as $1,000 and are quite bulky, therefore impractical for naturist photography.

Film needs to be shielded from the heat, so don't leave it in the glove compartment of your car. If you also tote a picnic cooler for drinks, put the film inside, sealed in a plastic zip-lock bag — away from the melting ice.

Depending upon the type of naturist photography you want to do, certain cameras are better suited than others. Polaroids are almost always a poor choice because the extreme contrast found at bright, sunny beaches is beyond the range of the film. Even cheap, plastic cameras (the kind often given away free with magazine subscriptions) loaded with 100 ISO color print film, will do a better job. If you insist on having instant prints, or giving them to people who pose for your "real" camera, shoot with fill-flash on overcast days.

Although a real beach camera (such as a Nikon Action-Touch or Nikonos) is a must for me, I packed a wide variety of other equipment during my recent tours of California's coastline. Right off the bat, I should make it clear I've never owned any high-tech, autofocus SLRs. I can't speak from experience, but I'm sure they'd do just fine — as long as you don't run out of batteries.

My tastes in equipment are simple, almost Spartan. When shooting candid, unposed photos, I prefer 35mm rangefinders since they're unobtrusive and harmless looking. Most people aren't intimidated by such "amateurish" gear, which makes them the right tool for capturing your friends and neighbors au naturel. For this type of photography, I have used a pocket-sized Olympus 35 RC, which offers both manual and auto exposure. Unfortunately, the camera, which was quite popular during the mid-1970s, hasn't been made since 1980. However, you might want to try to find one secondhand.

For action photos of someone frolicking in the surf or run-

ning along the shore, you can't beat the speed and versatility of a single lens reflex — just keep it away from sand and water. Here's one situation where a late-model autofocus SLR would have an advantage over an older, manual focus model.

Over the years, I've worked with many different Nikon camera models, including the original workhorse F, various Nikkormats, Nikon EL-2, FE and el cheapo EM. I currently use the FE-2 and FG models, with motor drives.

Except when I'm using fill-flash, I prefer the FGs because they're compact, offering both auto and manual exposure. Why would I choose a less expensive model for serious photography? Because when the inevitable "camera-in-the-drink" happens, I'll feel a whole lot better ruining a bargain-priced tool than a prestigious one.

For the same reason, I use two inexpensive, Series-E Nikkor zooms: the 36mm-72mm and 75mm-150mm. During summers

past, I've carried prime lenses ranging from 24mm to 300mm, but now I travel light and love it. Having "amateur" gear (which also gets the job done) makes it easier to work without screaming "pro" and attracting a lot of attention. Of course, you could also accomplish the same thing with a so-called "bridge camera," such as Canon's Sure Shot Zoom XL or Minolta's Freedom Zoom 90. Just make sure you keep 'em high and dry.

Regardless of what kind of equipment you use, protect it from thieves and out-of-orbit Frisbees. I once read about a famous pro who used a cheap styrofoam ice-chest to store thousands of dollars worth of cameras in the back seat of his Honda, which didn't have a trunk. He did it for years, without any problems. Coleman makes a compact padded cooler, designed to hold a six-pack, which costs less than $15. That's my beach-going camera bag.

Don't think you have to buy a camera manufacturer's lenses to get sharp pictures. There are a number of good independent companies such as Tokina, Kiron and Sigma, who can compete with the big boys. Personally, I've owned Tamron and Vivitar lenses and found them to be superb optically and an excellent value. On occasion, I still attach an inexpensive Vivitar teleconverter to my longer zoom when I need the extra reach of a lightweight, 300mm lens.

For more formal nude portraiture (a contradiction in terms?), I sometimes choose semi-private locales and switch to medium format cameras: a Bronica S-2A, with a 75mm f/2.8 Nikkor or a Yashica Mat 124-G, which can be used with fill-in flash at speeds up to 1/500 second because of its leaf shutter. In the past, I've also taken advantage of Bronica's SLR lenses, including the 40mm f/4 Nikkor and 150mm f/3.5 Zenzanon. When shooting with either camera under purely natural light, I use a tripod whenever possible to insure sturdy support and take full advantage of the larger 2¼" square negative size.

Until just a few years ago, my B&W film was invariably Tri-X. But now, Kodak's T-MAX offers finer grain, better sharpness and, to my tastes, longer tonal scale. It's ideal for nude beach photography! In the past, I rated Tri-X at 200 ISO (half its normal index) and reduced development accordingly in D-76, with good results. Now I do even better with T-MAX exposed at 400 and processed as recommended by Kodak in T-MAX developer. When it comes to color slide films, I prefer Kodachrome 64 and 200, depending upon the lighting conditions.

There are so many excellent color print films these days, I'd be hard-pressed to recommend a favorite. Kodak Ektar films are reputed to offer the finest grain and sharpness, but with

less exposure latitude than other films. This slim margin of error is a consideration if you use a point 'n' shoot camera which may lack the sophisticated metering system of a modern SLR.

Bright reflections from sun, sand and surf can fool your camera's light meter, resulting in underexposed pictures. So it's a real plus to have a model which allows some sort of manual override. If you're using color print film, don't hesitate to increase the exposure by at least a stop. Rest assured you have plenty of latitude: at least two under and two over, up to five stops! Be aware that today's color print films are so good,

if your pictures are too dark, too light or off-color, nine out of ten times it's the lab's fault. Return your unsatisfactory prints and make them do the job right!

B&W film isn't quite as forgiving, but there's still plenty of margin for error. With slide film, a half-stop may be enough, but for important pictures be sure to bracket your exposures.

Here's a trick to fool your auto-everything camera if it sets the film speed and won't allow adjustments: Cover the DX coding on the film cartridge with black tape and, in most cases, the camera will default to 100 ISO. Check the instruction manual to confirm this. By outsmarting your camera in this way, you can "overexpose" 200 ISO color print film and "underexpose" 64 ISO slide film exactly as I've suggested.

Although most amateur photographers don't think about using flash in bright sunlight, the built-in strobes on most auto-everything cameras really improve skinny-dipper photos, especially at midday when harsh shadows can ruin an otherwise good picture. Many times, waiting for the right light can mean the difference between an OK shot and a great one. Try

early mornings or late afternoons for the most flattering help from the sun: That's when swimwear photographers scramble to get their best images. In some locations, the "perfect" light may last only a few minutes, so you'll need both a discerning eye and quick reflexes.

If your SLR (such as Nikon's late, great FE-2) has a 1/250 second flash sync, you may want to experiment with fill-in flash

as well. Set the camera's exposure system on auto and the ASA speed of your TTL flash at two stops higher than the actual film speed and you'll lessen the "artificial" look outdoor flash pictures often have. Many top-of-the-line models, such as Canon's EOS-1 and Nikon's F4, do these calculations automatically. However, the idea of toting a $2,000 piece of equipment in a beach bag is frightening, to say the least!

A similar effect can be accomplished using any auto flash by manually setting the lens opening two stops smaller than recommended. In any case, make sure you stay within the sync range of your camera. On older models, this is often 1/60 second, limiting fill-flash to very slow films, overcast days or shots after sunset.

Another alternative is to use an older rangefinder or a twin lens reflex which will sync speeds up to 1/500. This can be quite inexpensive ($75 or less in the case of a secondhand Olympus RF or Yashica TLR) or priced out of this world (should you choose a late model Leica or Hasselblad).

Naturist photography doesn't always mean taking pictures of people without their clothes. What about strolling along in the buff, capturing other forms of natural beauty, such as the

shoreline, cliffs and waves? For this type of work, filters can add a spectacular touch.

Here are some examples: A polarizing filter can make white clouds really "pop" against blue sky. Graduated special effects "half and half" filters will brighten up color photography of dull sunsets.

For dramatic B&W photography, with dark skies and brilliant clouds, a red filter is essential. To lessen the effect, use orange or yellow. No matter what kind of film you have in your camera, a "cross-star" or "starburst" filter can turn the sun into a supernova, flaring out in all directions.

Filters are the least expensive photo accessories around, so don't be afraid to experiment. In addition to those produced by the camera manufacturers, Cokin, Vivitar, Hoya and Tiffen all make excellent glass.

If you're serious about improving your photography, there's no substitute for actually going out and taking pictures. Naturist photography has its own special problems and solutions which are best learned through experience. Using $500 worth of film with a little thought will go a lot farther to making you a better photographer than springing for a new camera.

CLOTHING-OPTIONAL
RESORTS & NATURIST CLUBS

Glen Eden Sun Club sits a little over an hour east of Los Angeles and claims to be California's largest clothing-optional retreat. Included in the sprawling grounds are indoor and outdoor pools, sauna, sports equipment and camping facilities. Glen Eden's calendar lists frequent sports and social events, so there's a good chance you'll find yourself in the middle of something exciting on almost any summer weekend. Write for their current schedule, P.O. Box 641, Corona, CA 91718, or dial (714) 277-4650 for more details.

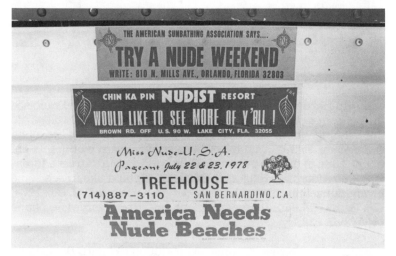

Elysium Fields, just 30 minutes from Los Angeles, was founded by Ed Lange, a veteran naturist promoter, photographer and publisher. In addition to lush grounds, the usual activities (volleyball, tennis, sauna, swimming pool, jacuzzi, etc.) and on-site parking for 200 cars, Elysium is best known for its New Age and alternative lifestyles workshops. Open every day, except Monday. "The Journal of the Senses," Elysium's quarterly bulletin, is available for $1/issue. Located at 814 Robinson Road, Topanga, CA 90290. Call (213) 455-1000 to visit as a guest.

Le Petit Chateau is a bed-and-breakfast inn which follows the au naturel tradition of the French Mediterranean. The perfect year-round getaway is located in America's winter playground at 1491 Via Soledad, Palm Springs, CA 92264. For reservations and room rates, call (619) 325-2686.

Lupin Naturist Club is just an hour's drive from San Francisco in the gorgeous Santa Cruz mountains. Nude tennis, volleyball, hot tubbing, swimming, dining and just plain relaxing are all on the agenda at this "family-oriented resort where clothing is optional." Site of the 1990 Naturist Gathering, Lupin's street address is 20600 Aldercraft Heights, Los Gatos. If you'd like to see some promotional literature or become a member, write P.O. Box 1274, Los Gatos, CA 95031. To arrange for an introductory visit, phone (408) 353-2250.

Naked City, owned by wheelchair-ridden sex guru Dick Drost, is a take-it-all-off strip club masquerading as a naturist resort. Several times a year, Naked City hosts beauty pageants ("Ms. Nude Hollywood," "Ms. Nude California," etc.) where pale-skinned, bleached blondes pose *Hustler* magazine style for horny truckers with Instamatics. A swimming pool, trampoline and X-rated video arcade complete this 20-acre "paradise." Admission for typical events is $30 for single men and $20 for couples, indicating women are in short supply. Naked City's mailing address is Box 2000, Homeland, CA 92348. They've also got a real cute phone number: (714) 926-BANG.

Olive Dell Ranch isn't as spacious as many Southern California nudist camps but it has all the trimmings. You won't find a friendlier bunch of people. Located at Route 1, Box 393, Colton, CA 92324. For better directions, call (714) 825-6619.

The Olympian Club sponsors indoor parties, picnics, camp-outs, beach visits and special events that make up a year-round social calendar for members. "One of the largest and oldest ASA travel clubs in the Western Region," claims their advertising, which also points out the nudist social group welcomes visitors from other ASA clubs. Want to join their next outing? Write P.O. Box 15277, North Hollywood, CA 91615. Need a quicker reply? Dial (213) 865-7371.

Raffles, a well-appointed naturist resort in Palm Springs, offers year-round journeys to Eden in a luxurious garden setting. Enjoy an in-the-buff Australian breakfast at poolside or soak away your troubles in the steamy spa. A heated pool, barbeque pits and suites with kitchens make this an ideal place to recharge your batteries and work on that perfect tan. For a free brochure or reservations, (619) 320-3949.

Treehouse II

Rawhide Ranch calls itself a "family nudist resort," offering swimming pools, a lake, various sports activities, a two-story entertainment center, camping and motel accommodations. If you've never stood in line for a restaurant hamburger in the nude, this is a good place to try it! The clothes-free facility is situated 20 miles from Sacramento at 8683 Rawhide Lane, Wilton, CA 95693. For more info on this American Sunbathing Association member, the number is (916) 687-6550.

The Sequoians is a large outdoor facility with the usual nudist camp amenities: a swimming pool, hot tub and volleyball along with tent and trailer campsites. Hiking, lots of grass and trees, BBQ grills, picnic tables, badminton and a sundeck complete the picture at this family-oriented fun spot. Drop by for a visit at 10200 Gull Canyon Road, Castro Valley, CA 94546, or dial (415) 582-0194 to see if the sun is shining.

Swallows/Sun Island offers a heated pool, sauna, jacuzzi, child's playground, a clubhouse, campsites, motel rooms and a restaurant. There's also plenty of friendly competition: volleyball, table tennis, shuffleboard and tennis, all played in the raw. To find out if they're really "The best for nude relaxation and recreation," pay them a visit at 1631 Harbison Canyon Road, El Cajon, CA 92019. For further directions, call (619) 445-3754.

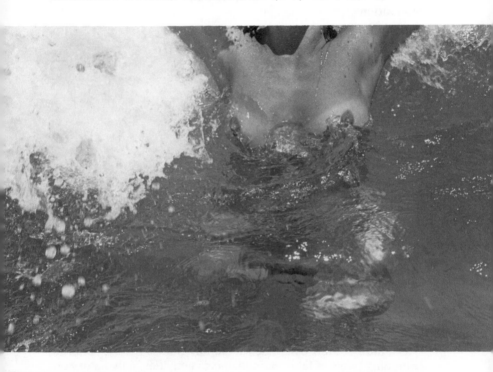

Treehouse Fun Ranch, home of a variety of beauty pageants as well as an in-the-buff chili cookoff, nude skydiving and other spectacular events, definitely lives up to its name. Tennis courts, heated pools, a sauna and spa, basketball, softball, ping-pong, horseshoes and volleyball are just some of the possible activities to enjoy like a jaybird. Did we forget to mention the restaurant, bar and video/pinball arcade? You can also take up year-round residence in the Treehouse's trailer park.

Certainly, one of its biggest attractions is that naturist photographers are permitted to use their cameras during special pre-pageant photo days. The Treehouse is 90 minutes east of Los Angeles at 17809 Glen Helen Road, Devore, CA 92407. To find out more, give owners Bill and Fran Flesher a ring at (714) 887-7056.

Treehouse Too Hotel Resort is a spinoff of the original Treehouse (see previous listing) located in ever-sunny Palm Springs. Guest amenities include complimentary beverages, breakfast and afternoon snacks, a heated pool and jacuzzi open 24 hours a day, cable TV with HBO and ESPN, air-conditioning and outdoor cool misting during summer months. 10% discounts for ASA and Naturist Society members. Conveniently located in the heart of town at 1466 N. Palm Canyon Drive, Palm Springs, CA 92262. For more information or room reservations, call (619) 322-9431.

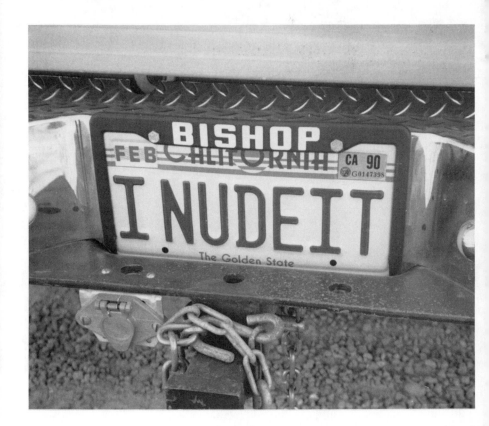

The wilds of Berkeley's Tilden Park

OF INTEREST TO NATURISTS: RECOMMENDED PUBLICATIONS & VIDEOS

Bare In Mind, "A Nudist News Service," has been an excellent source of up-to-the-minute free beach information since 1972. The monthly tabloid-sized publication uncovers the skinny-dipping scene with photos, cartoons, interviews and feature articles on the current state of undress in the Southland and beyond. Subscriptions to *Bare In Mind* (P.O. Box 368, Perris, CA 92370) are $23/year.

California Coastal Access Guide , published by the California Coastal Commission, has detailed, easy-to-read maps covering the entire shoreline from Del Norte County and the Oregon border, south to San Diego. Although only a handful of sites are acknowledged as "official" nude beaches, this information-packed (288 pages), well-illustrated volume is invaluable when used with other sources. Of special interest are the descriptions of facilities, local history and environment. If you're serious about combing the coast — with or without your clothes — don't leave home without it. The 1983 "Expanded Edition" costs $10.95, a terrific bargain. You may also want to purchase its 384-page Big Brother, the *California Coastal Resource Guide*. First published in 1987 for $14.95, it provides an even closer look and better photos, including a cover shot by Ansel Adams.

Bay view from Marin County

Great Hot Springs of the West, first written by Bill Kaysing back in 1974 (revised and expanded in 1990), is still considered a classic. More than 40 California hot spots are listed and photographed, with similar uncoverage of Arizona, Colorado, Idaho, Montana, New Mexico, Nevada, Oregon, Utah, Washington and Wyoming. Whether you prefer little-known, primitive hideaways or luxurious commercial accommodations, this book will help you find just the right place to soak your bones. $14.95 from Capra Press, P.O. Box 2068, Santa Barbara, CA 93120.

Heritage Video is a company with a worldwide focus on nudism, with tapes from Holland, Africa, New Zealand and California. Scenes of body painting from San Diego's Black's Beach, a nude boat party on San Francisco Bay, naked skydiving and a chili cook-off at the Treehouse Fun Ranch near San Bernardino are all part of the clothes-free West Coast footage. You can order by phone (prices range from $39.95 to $59.95, Visa and MasterCard accepted) from Heritage Video: (714) 522-7070. Their mailing address is P.O. Box 4447, Whittier, CA 90607.

Hot Springs and Hot Pools of the U.S., by Jayson Loam, David Bybee and Marjorie Gersh, is an expanded rewrite of Loam's original book "Hot Springs and Pools of the Southwest." The trio's first nationwide edition, published by Aqua Thermal Access in 1990, includes hundreds of hot-water hangouts, from Florida to

Maine, to Southern California and Washington. Not surprisingly, the Golden State ranks #1 in exposure with 65 pages of maps, photos and listings. At your favorite bookstore for $17.95, or through Aqua Thermal Access, 3100 Erin Lane, Santa Cruz, CA 95065. You may also want to subscribe to Jayson Loam's spin-off, "Aqua Thermal Access Journal," which updates "Hot Springs and Hot Pools of the U.S." and gives informal personal reports on hot springs hub-and-spoke vacations, hot tubbing tips and more. A one-year subscription (three issues) is $5 from P.O. Box 91, Soquel, CA 95073.

North American Guide to Nude Recreation is a nudist park directory published by the American Sunbathing Association (ASA). It features outstanding naturist photography (over 400 shots!) by, among others, the late Jerry Derbyshire. Several California clubs are highlighted, including Glen Eden, Lupin, Silver Valley, Swallows Sun Island and Treehouse Too. Available at your ASA clubs everywhere or postpaid for $18.95 (plus $3 shipping) from The Naturist Store, P.O. Box 132, Oshkosh, WI 54902. For more information, contact the American Sunbathing Association directly: (407) 933-2064.

Nude & Natural uncovers all the bases as a quarterly magazine which serves as The Naturist Society's principal forum. Created by true believers in the benefits of clothes-free living, a typical issue discusses ways to gain acceptance of public nudity, how to deal with gawkers and reports on the legal standings of nude beaches around the globe. There are also reviews of naturist books and videotapes. If you can't decide between viewing "Natural Summer" by Edin and Ethel Velez or "The Forest of Life" by Mike Herring, *Nude & Natural* can help.

The editorial photos are sometimes amateurish, but often quite beautiful, and no one will ever accuse Managing Editor Lee Baxandall of trying to sell magazines by using pictures of pretty young women. Many of the color covers have featured average-looking couples and middle-aged men.

N&N also updates Baxandall's excellent "World Guide to Nude Beaches and Recreation" (see listing below). Single copies are $6 (plus $3 shipping); non-Naturist Society member subscriptions are $25/year. Send your check or money order to The Naturists, P.O. Box 132, Oshkosh, WI 54902.

San Francisco Bay Guardian is a free, weekly alternative newspaper that has published a great nude beach guide every summer since 1976. Compiled by well-known freelance writer Gary Hanauer, the *Guardian*'s detailed information on "Northern California's distinctive natural resources" is definitely a keeper. However, the flimsy newsprint isn't likely to hold up for more than a few

trips to the beach, so be sure to pick up at least two copies while they're on the stands. If all else fails, you can order back issues for $3. Send your check or money order to Bay Guardian, 520 Hampshire Street, San Francisco, CA 94110.

Spectator magazine may be considered too outrageous and/or sexually explicit by many card-carrying naturists, but this offshoot of the now-defunct *Berkeley Barb* — the original underground newspaper — thrives in the 1990s by battling censorship, fighting the AIDS epidemic with health information and writing about nude beaches. In fact, excerpts from this book first appeared in the pages of *Spectator*.

Back issues are not available, but if you live within California, subscriptions are $29 a year, or $15 for six months. You can also pick up a copy at hundreds of newsstands and bookstores from San Diego to Reno. *Spectator*'s mailing address is P.O. Box 1984, Berkeley, CA 94701.

World Guide to Nude Beaches and Recreation is a gorgeous catalog of skinny-dipping sites from Antarctica to New Zealand. A feast of information and visuals, author Lee Baxandall's master-work became an instant classic when it was first published in 1980. A grand new edition is in the works, scheduled to hit the stands in 1991, but as of this writing, no cover price has been set. The 1983 Harmony Books edition, out of print for several years, was $14.95.

Although only a small part of the book deals with California's bare-bottomed beaches, you'll be impressed by the amount of research that went into this exhaustive exploration. If you don't see it at your favorite bookseller, contact The Naturist Store, P.O. Box 132, Oshkosh, WI 54902.

Panther Beach near Santa Cruz

CLOTHES-FREE
COMMUNITY RESOURCES

T he best things in life are free, but sometimes you've got to work (or fight) hard to keep them. Knowing this, naturists concerned with protecting their rights have put together political action groups and information centers. Donations and volunteer input are always welcome.

Every effort has been made to insure the accuracy of these listings. Although the addresses and phone numbers were correct at press time, be aware that some naturist organizations are non-profit, one-person operations, which may unplug or relocate at any time.

Au Naturel is a Southern California-based group which can fill you in on what's happening at nude beaches between San Diego and Santa Barbara. For more details, call (818) 895-1654, or write Au Naturel, P.O. Box 323, Reseda, CA 91337.

Bare In Mind, "A Nudist News Service," has been an excellent source of up-to-the-minute free beach information since 1972. The monthly tabloid-sized publication uncovers the world of skinny-dipping with photos, cartoons, interviews and feature articles on the current state of undress in the Southland and beyond. Subscriptions to *Bare In Mind* (P.O. Box 368, Perris, CA 92370) are $23/year.

Bay Area Naturist Network, is one of the many teams nationwide battling for clothing-optional rights. They can provide a status report on the dozens of sans swimsuit locales around San Francisco. A self-addressed, stamped envelope to P.O. Box 6221, Albany, CA 94706 should get you a quick reply.

BeachFront USA is a naturist newspaper for those interested in the nude beach scene throughout California and the rest of the country. For a one-year subscription, send $15 to BeachFront USA, P.O. Box 328, Moreno Valley, CA 92337.

Black's Beach Bares Association will add you to their newsletter list for $10/year. San Diego area residents, or anyone who has enjoyed California's most famous nude beach would do well to support this clothing-optional club. Address all inquiries to P.O. Box 12255, LaJolla, CA 92039.

Camping Bares of San Diego sponsors activities for nude recreation throughout Southern California. A long-standing supporter (since the seventies) of clothes-free adventures and pioneering, the Camping Bares have been credited as being a "... gregarious, earthy bunch" by "World Guide" author Lee Baxandall, who also claims they publish a "great newsletter." For more info, send a self-addressed, stamped envelope to P.O. Box 81589, San Diego, CA 92138-1589. If you can't wait for the mails, dial (619) 689-9374.

Central California Beachfront is a small grassroots organization located in the heart of the Golden State's year-round sun-worshipping territory. If you've got questions about the nude beach scene from San Luis Obispo to Santa Barbara, these are the people to ask. You can write them at P.O. Box 351, Lompoc, CA 93438.

College Cove Naturists focuses its energy on one of California's most beautiful buff bathing locales: College Cove, 25 miles north of Eureka. This well-organized group can also give you the no-clothes lowdown on nearby Baker's Beach and other sunning sites in the area. If you request information or their newsletter, be sure to include a small donation with your self-addressed, stamped envelope: College Cove Naturists, c/o Douglas Beck, 2340 Fairfield St., Eureka, CA 95501. Or call the College Cove hotline, (707) 443-2639.

The main entrance to Garrapata Beach

Friends of Garrapata Beach are currently involved in preserving the nude traditions of what many consider to be the most spectacular skinny-dipping site in the Monterey/Big Sur area. Acquired in 1988 by the California park system, advocates fear the planned construction of fences, a paved parking area and restrooms will draw hordes of clothed tourists, eventually resulting in a ban on nudity. To find out the current state of affairs, send a self-addressed stamped envelope to P.O. Box 1010, Pacific Grove, CA 93950.

Friends of Pirate's Cove hope to protect the central coast's crown jewel for buff bathing, Pirate's Cove near San Luis Obispo. Although the hills overlooking the beach have already been slated for development in the form of homes and condos, no ground has been broken yet. If you haven't already visited Pirate's Cove, spending an afternoon there will convince you this is a beach worth fighting for. Curious about how you can help? Get in touch with Friends of Pirate's Cove, 1251 Sage Street, Arroyo Grande, CA 93420. If you need a more speedy reply, dial (805) 481-9352.

Nudist Information Center, hosted by Suzy Davis, concerns itself with upcoming naturist events and the current legal standing of clothes-free sites throughout California. They offer "The Nudist Passport" entitling members to a long list of fringe benefits, including subscriptions to *Bare in Mind* and *Nude & Natural*. Give Suzy a call if you're interested in becoming a part of the nude wave: (619) 254-2500. You can also write the Nudist Information Center at P.O. Box 512, Daggett, CA 92327.

The Naturists, Inc. is the Mercedes Benz of nudist organizations. It houses several operations under one roof, including The Naturist Society, Free Beaches Documentation Center and *Nude & Natural* (formerly *Clothed With the Sun*), a quarterly magazine packed with articles on every aspect of clothes-free living. "*N & N* policy encourages a diversity and debate of values, the better to combat inoperative and self-destructive tendencies within the clothes-optional community of social change," explains Managing Editor Lee Baxandall.

N & N also features excellent photography and "The Naturist Network," an indispensable guide to dozens of nude recreational facilities, social and political organizations and clothing-optional contacts across the country and around the world. Everything from Jest For Fun Juggers to Opera Buffs, Gay & Lesbian Naturists, Mensa Nudists and the American Sunbathing Association can be found in their exhaustive listings.

The long-awaited update of Baxandall's "World Guide To Nude Beaches and Recreation," tagged as the "skinny-dipper's bible" when it was last published by Harmony Books in 1983, will be brought back to life by The Naturists, Inc. Look for the nude and improved edition in Summer 1991.

The Naturist Store sells a wide variety of books, magazines and videotapes, as well as official Naturist Society T-shirts, towels and other accessories by mail.

You can become part of the best thing that's happened to nude recreation since suntan lotion by sending $30 to The Naturists, Inc., P.O. Box 132, Oshkosh, Wisconsin 54902. Membership includes a one-year subscription to *Nude & Natural*, as well as special discounts on Naturist products and services.

River Dippers, a family-oriented group based in the California capital, have spent many a hot summer afternoon exploring the Sacramento Delta and beyond as God intended. If you'd like to explore the wilds of Central and Northern California in the flesh, send a self-addressed, stamped envelope to P.O. Box 2693, Sacramento, CA 95812 and ask for their five-page set of guidesheets.

Russian River Naturists know the nooks and crannies of Sonoma County's clothes-free inland empire. Since the area occasionally has problems with anti-nudity enforcement, you might want to check with them before baring your buns at Wohler Bridge or Camp Meeker. Address your questions on the area to Steve Charmaz, 1163 Hooper Avenue #17, Santa Rosa, CA 95401 or call (707) 523-3114.

Sanrobles, Inc. Nudist Travel Club hits the highway in pursuit of bare-bottomed recreation throughout Northern California. A great way to socialize and see the San Francisco Bay Area in a whole nude light! Contact P.O. Box 4763, Hayward, CA 94540.

South Bay Naturists, led by Rich Pasco, have coordinated annual beach cleanups at Bonny Doon near Santa Cruz since 1987. *South Bay Naturist News,* the group's newsletter, informs its readers about emerging nude beaches and topics of special interest to those who enjoy the clothes-free lifestyle. In addition, members enjoy a lively social calendar: nude barbecues, visits to bare-bottomed resorts (such as Lupin Naturist Club in Los Gatos) and more. To volunteer as a nude garbage person or just get in on the fun, write P.O. Box 23781, San Jose, CA 95153.

Paradise Lost? No way, thanks to illustrator Rob Harper's easy-to-read maps of the Golden State's principal nude beach sectors: Southern California, Central Coast, San Francisco Bay Area, North Coast and Lake Tahoe. Although the directions following each listing should be enough to get you there, refer to your favorite beach by number for further clarification.

© RMH 1988

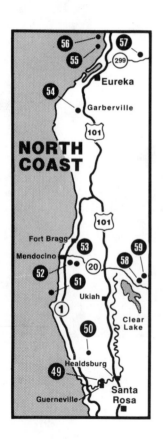

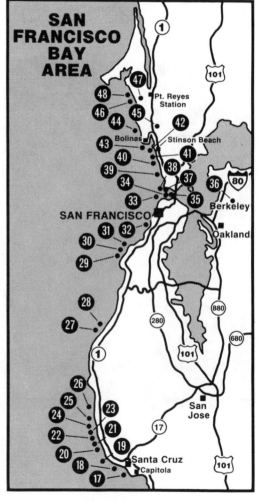

NORTH COAST

LAKE TAHOE AREA

SAN FRANCISCO BAY AREA

CENTRAL COAST

SOUTHERN CALIFORNIA

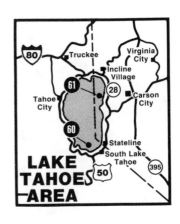

80

Truckee

Virginia City

Incline Village

28

Carson City

Tahoe City

61

60

Stateline

South Lake Tahoe

50

395

LAKE TAHOE AREA

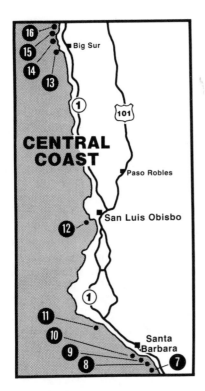

16

15

14

13

Big Sur

1

101

CENTRAL COAST

Paso Robles

12

San Luis Obisbo

1

11

10

9

8

7

Santa Barbara

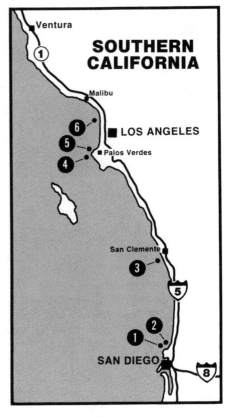

Ventura

1

SOUTHERN CALIFORNIA

Malibu

6

5

4

LOS ANGELES

Palos Verdes

San Clemente

3

5

2

1

SAN DIEGO

8

Photography: Colleen McEvoy

ABOUT THE AUTHOR

Dave Patrick has spent almost two decades photographing and writing about California's nude beaches. His work has appeared in more than 300 newspapers and magazines, including *Playboy, Rolling Stone, Hustler, High Times, BAM, Creem, Nude & Natural, Bare In Mind, Health & Efficiency, San Francisco Bay Guardian* and the late, great *Berkeley Barb*.

The former Navy photographer's mate (discharged after 10 months as a conscientious objector) has lived in the San Francisco Bay Area since 1973. In addition to credits on numerous posters, calendars, travel books and album covers, Dave's photography is featured in the skinny-dipper's bible, Lee Baxandall's "World Guide To Nude Beaches And Recreation." As a rock 'n' roll photographer during the 1970s he did promotional shots for radio station KSAN, Jefferson Starship, Frank Zappa and The Tubes.

Since 1980, Patrick has been principal lensman for the legendary Exotic-Erotic Halloween and New Year's Eve Balls. He's currently Renegade Editor and Chief Photographer for *Spectator* magazine. An avid bowler, Dave rolled three ABC-sanctioned perfect games during the 1989–90 season when he averaged 216 in two different leagues.